Fleeing God

Fleeing

Fear, Call, and the Book of Jonah

God

Tara Soughers

COWLEY PUBLICATIONS

Lanham, Chicago, New York, Toronto, and Plymouth, UK

Published by Cowley Publications
An imprint of Rowman & Littlefield Publishers, Inc.
A wholly owned subsidiary of The Rowman & Littlefield Publishing Group, Inc.
4501 Forbes Boulevard, Suite 200
Lanham, MD 20706

Estover Road
Plymouth PL6 7PY
United Kingdom

Distributed by National Book Network

Scripture quotations are taken from The New Revised Standard Version
of the Bible, © 1989, by the Division of Christian Education of the
National Council of the Churches of Christ in the United States
of America. Used by permission.

Library of Congress Cataloging-in-Publication Data

Soughers, Tara, 1961–
    Fleeing God : fear, call, and the book of Jonah / Tara Soughers.
      p. cm.
    ISBN-13: 978-1-56101-295-4 (pbk. : alk. paper)
    ISBN-10: 1-56101-295-5 (pbk. : alk. paper)
    1. Bible. O.T. Jonah—Criticism, interpretation, etc. I. Title.
    BS1605.52.S68 2007
    224'.9206—dc22   2007009656

Printed in the United States of America.

♾™ The paper used in this publication meets the minimum requirements of
American National Standard for Information Sciences—Permanence of
Paper for Printed Library Materials, ANSI/NISO Z39.48-1992.

❊ Contents ❊

Acknowledgments

MY pursuit of the big fish has not been a solitary venture. I have been blessed by many people, and through their words and actions, I have come to understand my call more deeply.

I give thanks for my family. Mike, Arielle, and Gregory remind me daily of my call to love and be loved.

I give thanks for all those who have helped me in the preparation of this manuscript. I thank my husband, Mike, who made sure that initial manuscript was presentable. I thank the Rev. Edward Coolidge who read that manuscript and gave me invaluable suggestions. I give thanks to Ulrike Guthrie, who edited the final manuscript and pushed me to produce a better book.

Finally I give thanks for all those, who through the years have shared stories of their calls, and those, who like Martha have been the voice of God to me.

To all my companions on the way to Nineveh
and those who have shared their fish stories with me.

☀ Introduction ☀

I WISH I could say that my relationship with God is always full of brightness and light. I wish I could say that I have always been eager to grow closer to God. I wish I could say that obedience to God's will is something that I have always found easy. But I can't. My journey has been filled with peaks and valleys, bright sunshine and impenetrable darkness. There have been times when I have eagerly moved forward, and times when I have been pushed along kicking and screaming. If my growth in the knowledge and love of God had been due solely to my own efforts, my progress would have been much slower. God's grace has nourished and nurtured me, even when I didn't particularly want to grow.

If I have learned anything on this journey, it is this: God doesn't give up on us, even when we deserve it. That is at least one of the messages of the book of Jonah. Even at our most unlovable, God is acting to transform us into the people whom we were created to be (whether we want to be transformed or not!). God loves us, in spite of ourselves.

Throughout my journey, I have been nurtured and supported by scripture. At different times, different pieces of scripture have spoken to me, enlightening my path and guiding me in the way that I needed to go. Through these pieces, God has spoken to me and shaped me.

The book of Jonah was an important piece of scripture to me as I struggled with my call to ordained ministry. Like Jonah, I was being called to something that conflicted with the plans that I had made for my own life. Like Jonah, I initially tried to flee, rather than follow what God was calling me to do. Like Jonah, my attempts to flee were unsuccessful, and in the process I was changed—not made perfect, but closer to the person God intends me to be.

You may not have been called to ordained ministry. Nonetheless, I suspect that there have been times in your life when you also have felt called to do something that you didn't want to do. Perhaps it was inconvenient. Maybe it seemed absolutely impossible. Or, like in Jonah's case, it might have been simply repugnant. The calls that we hear are not always the ones that we would have liked to hear.

Several years ago, we moved to a new state. My husband, Mike, and I had two small children. His intention had been to find part-time work, but with the high cost of daycare, we could not afford for him to work part-time. His choices were either to work full-time or to stay at home with the children. He had never imagined himself as a stay-at-home father, and yet for several years, that was his call.

I invite you, as you read this book, to reflect upon the calls that you have heard: both those to which you said yes and those you tried to avoid. I suspect that if they were really calls from God, you were changed in some way by the experience, much as Jonah was and much as I have been changed. Calls, whether they are to some grand work or to some quieter, less obvious ministry, do not leave us untouched. We are marked by our calls.

I do not know what you have been called to do by God, and I do not know what God will call you to do in the future.

Only God knows. What I do know is that God is always call-ing each of us to continue in that journey ever closer into the heart of Christ. By God's grace, we are being transformed.

I suggest that you read the book of Jonah through before you begin this book, in order to get the story firmly in mind. You will probably also wish to keep the story of Jonah on hand as you read through this book, in order to compare what I have written with the original. At the beginning of each chap-ter, I have cited the corresponding portion of the book of Jonah to make comparisons easier.

My reflections come from my own experiences. The book of Jonah may speak to you in a different way. It may be that God has a different set of lessons in mind for you. If it prompts you to think about your own experiences in fleeing from God, my writing will have been worthwhile. As Jonah discovered, however, we can't actually flee God, no matter how much we might wish to do so.

Chapter 1

Call and Jonah

BEHIND the dining room table were shelves with a variety of knickknacks. A surprising number seemed to be of whales. Moving closer to examine the collection, my eye was caught by a beautiful crystal whale with a small man inside—Jonah in the belly of the whale. The little glass whale was a work of art, one among several whales with Jonahs inside. I was impressed by the artistry, but I had no idea then how much that story would come to mean to me.

Before that day, the story of Jonah was simply a story that I had learned long ago in Sunday School but which was scarcely believable as I grew older. It was not until later that I would come to see the parallels between myself and the reluctant prophet of Gath-hepher, between my life and his. Although I did not receive a call to preach to the people of Nineveh, the idea of my being called to the priesthood seemed no more believable to me than being called to preach to Nineveh had to Jonah.

At the time, I was a graduate student in biochemistry, struggling with the direction that my life was going to take. The research work that I had been doing was not going well. In fact, the project on which I had been working had come to a dead end. Such dead ends are not unusual problems in a research laboratory, but they are deadly for thesis writing. To continue, I would need to start over completely with a brand new project, leaving behind all of my previous work. In addition, a low grade in a required course meant that I was in danger of being dropped from the graduate program altogether.

I felt adrift. Originally, I had been filled with great enthusiasm about the course my life was taking, but at that point, it no longer inspired me with the passion that had been a part of my earlier journey. I was also considering other alternatives, but none seemed any more attractive. I thought that perhaps I might become a photographer instead, and I had enrolled in a correspondence course, but even that seemed uninspiring.

Martha, the owner of the glass whale, was a member of the church that I had been attending. Knowing of my current unhappiness with the direction my life was taking, she invited me over to talk. At that point, I was willing to talk to anyone who might be able to help me. For some time, we sat in her dining room amid the Jonah collection and discussed various possibilities open to me: continuing with biochemistry, becoming a photographer, or doing something else altogether. Eventually the conversation trailed off with no resolution, and I sat there, as miserable as I had been when I came. It all seemed so hopeless.

After a time of silence, Martha leaned forward over the table and said, "What you really want to be is a priest."

I was shocked. For about a year, that same idea had kept coming up in my thoughts. For a year, I had ruthlessly pushed it down. It was too late: I was already in the middle of a Ph.D. program in biochemistry. In addition, I was a failure: I had almost flunked out of my graduate program because of my difficulties with one course. I could not possibly be called to be a priest, for God deserved only the best. How could a failure be called to be a priest?

There were a variety of ways in which I could have responded to the call rising so insistently within me, but my response was denial. I denied the call welling up in me, determined to make it go away by refusing to allow it into the light of day. For a year, I had mentioned it to no one. For a whole year, I had explored other options, refusing to listen to the one option that kept resurfacing.

The call, however, was not content simply to well up within me. If I could not hear what it was saying in my own heart, then perhaps I could hear it in the voice of another.

My first response to Martha was disbelief. There was no way that she could have known of this crazy notion, for I had told no one. I had not yet learned that calls cannot be denied so easily, nor that God often uses others to prod us into doing what we are called to do. Calls are not simply private matters between God and us, as I was to discover. They need the support, validation, and occasionally prodding of others to come to full life.

Seated across the table from her, I tried to deny it, but I suspect my initial response gave me away. My secret was out, and it was demanding a response. I could answer the call with a yes or with a no, but denial was no longer an option.

Before I left, Martha lent me one of the whales with Jonah inside to take home for a while. As she reminded me, the tale of Jonah teaches many lessons, but one lesson is quite clear. If God is calling us to Nineveh, we will—somehow—end up in Nineveh, whether we want to go there or not.

<<

As my wise mentor had suggested, God eventually did make sure that I got to Nineveh.

It seemed that I struggled against my call every bit as hard as Jonah had. Then, when I finally capitulated and headed for my Nineveh, I—like Jonah—had definite ideas about the results of following the call. Like Jonah, I also found out that God had some surprises planned, and that not all of them were to my liking.

In the Episcopal tradition that formed me, we profess that all people are made ministers at their baptisms. Each and every one of us has a call. We are called to carry on Christ's work of reconciliation in the world. That is the call that encompasses all other calls. To do this, we are to "seek and serve Christ in all persons, loving your neighbor as yourself."[1] Each of us is called to live out our personal calls in the larger context of this call to Christian life.

I have had many calls in my lifetime. In addition to being called as a priest, I was also called to be a wife and to be a mother. At various times, I followed yet other calls. I was a student and a research scientist. Some of my calls have been to long-term ministries (certainly marriage, parenthood, and writing qualify as long-term). Others have been one time or short-term calls. Sitting in a hospital room, rocking an infant so that the mother could leave to take a shower, was definitely a short-term call, but important nonetheless. Providing a shoulder to cry upon, a hug when needed, even a smile: these are also calls we follow each and every day. Other calls are life changing.

So what do I mean when I talk about call? I like Frederick Buechner's definition of call as the intersection of our passions and the world's needs,[2] for I believe that call is about passion. A call evokes strong emotions within us. A call can be strongly attractive, or as in the case of Jonah strongly repellent, but we are never left neutral in the face of a call from

God. Call is the Holy Spirit within us stirring up the waters, and because of that, calls can be born out of great personal turmoil. Calls can turn our world, or at least our expectations, upside down. It is not easy, however, to banish a true call, for it will continue to haunt us. Unfulfilled calls are often the things that we regret not doing for the rest of our lives.

Passion by itself is no guarantee of call, for we can become passionate about something for reasons other than the movement of God in our lives. We may be hoping to become famous. We may crave excitement. We may be hoping to find love. All of these desires may be mistaken for God's call. It is all too easy to convince ourselves that what we would like to do is what we are called to do. How many of us, as children, were convinced that we would be the next Nobel prize–winning scientist, a cowboy, a superstar, the president of the United States, or the greatest football player ever? At that point, we would have been convinced that was indeed what God meant us to be. This is where the second part of Buechner's definition comes in. Somehow this call must also address some need in our world. We are meant to be of service. We are meant to reach out to our troubled and broken world, and the ways in which we are called to do that may be nothing like we imagined as children. They may be a whole lot less spectacular.

Most of us do not have the power and resources to fix the major problems of the world. By ourselves, we are not able to ensure that all have enough to eat. Our call, however, may be to start a food pantry, or volunteer in a soup kitchen, or support development work in Africa. By ourselves, we are not able to cure AIDS. Our call may instead be to befriend someone living with AIDS, or to work in AIDS education, or to provide the necessary resources so that AIDS orphans may go to school. We are not able to provide housing for everyone who needs it. Our call may instead be to work with others in our communities to lobby for subsidized housing, or to work on a house for Habitat for Humanity, or to volunteer in a homeless shelter. A call responds to a need, and responding to the needs of others helps us to keep our calls grounded in reality.

When I was in junior high school, I went to Haiti with a group called VOSH, Volunteer Optometric Services to Humanity. This group of optometrists gathered glasses that people no longer needed and determined the prescription. They then traveled to countries, such as Haiti, where optometric services were not available. After a free eye examination, they provided a pair of glasses that fit the person. For many of the Haitians, this was the only opportunity to get the help they needed, and many walked days and waited hours in the sun for the possibility of seeing better. I saw in these optometrists a call to use their skills and training to help others.

A call not only helps others: it changes us as well, as Jonah learned. We cannot be called and remain unchanged—whether we accept the call or reject it. As Jacob learned in the book of Genesis, encounters with God leave us forever marked.[3] They cause us to grow into the people that God desires.

Growth is not easy. Often difficult and painful, it requires us to change, to leave behind the identities that we have forged. It requires risking everything that is most important to us.

Although it is true that there are times when we embrace our calls with great enthusiasm, there are many other times when we do not. The Bible is full of examples of people who respond to calls with reluctance, skepticism, and even flight.

Moses cited other people's disbelief and his own lack of elo-quence as reasons for not originally accepting his call.[4]

When the call comes announced by an angel, often the first thing that the angel says is "Do not be afraid." It could be that the angel says this because angels (unlike their popu-lar depictions) are quite scary looking. I suspect that their message is actually the scariest thing about them. When they appear it means that life is about to be turned upside down.

Having encountered a few scary calls in my own life, I can see myself in Jonah's story. At such times, it seems that the most reasonable response to a call is to flee as far as I can in the other direction. Unfortunately, as Jonah discovered, no matter how far we flee, we cannot leave God behind. God will make sure that eventually we get to Nineveh, even if it takes something as preposterous as a very big fish to get us there.

Chapter 2

Fish Stories

JONAH is a fish story, a very big fish story. Because of that, it is easy to dismiss it as only a fable.

Fish stories, in our culture, have a reputation for being tall tales. One is almost expected to exaggerate fish stories, and because of that no one takes them very seriously. Jonah is often seen in a similar way, as a cute story that did not really happen. His story is simply a fishy tall tale, not fit for serious adult consideration. It is suitable only for entertainment for children (with a satisfactory moral attached).

We can also dismiss Jonah by trying to make his story logical and reasonable. We can argue about whether Jonah was swallowed by a whale (anatomically impossible) or by some other type of big fish. We can try to find out what kind of fish would be large enough to swallow Jonah whole, and yet spit him out apparently unharmed three days later. We can debate whether or not this is all really possible. On the way, we miss the whole point of the story.

For the story of Jonah really, truly is a fish story, a story that cannot be proven, a story that seems unlikely or even impossible. So why was this story kept? Probably for the same reasons that the rest of the material in the Bible was kept: it conveys something deeply true about the nature of God and the nature of human beings. It was kept because that story, as improbable as it is, helps us understand something that bare statements and laws cannot convey.

Stories have a power all of their own. They illuminate reality in ways that facts often cannot. They change people's perceptions and lives. Through stories we pass along our values and traditions and histories. Well aware that spiritual matters could not be easily comprehended in discursive speech, Jesus told stories instead. In fact, Matthew insists that Jesus told them nothing except in stories.[5]

So stories may be profoundly true, without being factual. For me, the stories of the Bible are true, even if I can never prove that they are factual. I may not ever know whether it was a big fish or a whale that swallowed Jonah. I may not even know whether Jonah himself actually existed, but there is truth in the story nonetheless.

In the film *Big Fish*, Will Bloom is estranged from his father but returns home as his father is dying. The cause of their estrangement is literally a big fish story, or rather a whole series of fish stories that leave Will frustrated. Because of the obviously exaggerated nature of his father's claims, Will rejects all of the stories and ultimately his father as well. In the course of the movie, the son is surprised to learn that these stories do contain some fact. Even more surprising, they contain a great deal of truth. In the end, Will understands what his mother had claimed: that through the stories, the truth of his father was indeed revealed.

So come with me and explore the deep truth of this big fish story. In the end, it does not really matter what kind of fish swallowed Jonah. Instead, explore with me what truth is in this fish story, for in this improbable tale, God is speaking.

Once upon a time there was a man and there was a big fish. . . .

Chapter 3

Jonah, Son of Amittai, From Gath-hepher

Jonah 1:1–3

ONCE upon a time, long, long ago, in a land far away. . . .
No, that is how fairy tales begin, and fairy tales often are
a little vague. True fish stories have details, because details
make a story more exciting. What fisherman or woman, when
telling the story, leaves out the place and the time of the great
catch or the length of the fish? Good fish stories require
details, and the story of Jonah is no exception.

We begin with a character, one Jonah by name. Already
there is some specificity, but the author is not content with
leaving it at that. It is a specific Jonah, Jonah who is the son
of Amittai. That could just be a rhetorical flourish, but the
name of Jonah, the son of Amittai, is not unknown in the
Bible. According to 2 Kings, Jonah, the son of Amittai, was a
prophet who supported King Jeroboam in restoring the bor-
ders of Israel.[6]

This puts a whole different spin on the story. It becomes
not simply a fable about anyone, but a story about a particular character who lived in a particular time, some seven to

eight hundred years BCE, and in a particular place called Gath-hepher.

Such details make fish stories much more interesting and more believable. Real names and real places support the facts of the story. We know that Jonah existed, from the reference in 2 Kings. Gath-hepher was real place, a known village in Galilee. The details add plausibility.

But maybe such details serve another purpose in this account. What do they tell us about such calls? Why is it important that we know exactly whom it was that God called? Does it really matter that his name was Jonah? Does it really matter that he was the son of Amittai, or that he came from Gath-hepher?

I think it does. A call (like a good fish story) is very specific and full of details. I'm not talking about those general calls to us to grow in our relationship to God, those calls to live righteous and holy lives. I am talking about those calls that are uniquely ours.

The story of Jonah is not about living a generally holy life. It is not about being a moral person in general. This is a story about one particular man, in one particular place, at one particular time, struggling with what God was calling him (and no one else) to do.

Each of us is likewise the product of a specific set of parents. Each of us comes from a particular place. These details are of vital importance to our unique identities. Jonah was who he was because he was the son of Amittai. Jonah was who he was precisely because he came from Gath-hepher. And it was because of who he was that Jonah was called to Nineveh.

Our calls, like Jonah's, do not come simply as bolts out of the blue (although occasionally it may seem that way). Instead, our calls are integrally tied up with who we are. In answering them we grow fully into the people God has created us to be.

When I am preparing youth for confirmation, I ask them to do a service project. That, in itself, is not unusual, but I instruct them to find something that uses their particular gifts and talents. Athletic abilities led to charity softball games and bike-a-thons. Musical talents enriched worship and delighted the homeless. Nursing home residents were treated to manicures and bingo games. People were fed, clothed, and provided Christmas presents for their children. Prayer beads were made and distributed. Talent shows raised money for charity. A blood drive was organized. People were educated about homelessness. Rooms were painted and decorated, and Sunday School programs were enriched. Each year, I am amazed and awed by the variety of ways in which God's call is expressed in those youth.

We may at times wish for some generic call. Looking at other people's lives, we may envy them in their circumstances. Their lives may seem more peaceful or successful or simply easier. We may wish that we could trade our lives for theirs. We might long for God to call us in the same way that God had called them.

Calls, though, are not interchangeable any more than lives are interchangeable. God calls each of us to our own specific ministries, based not on who we would like to be but on who we really are. God calls me—Tara, daughter of Peggy and Dick, raised in a small town in Indiana—to one task, and God calls you to another. There is no one like me or like you, and because of that no two people's calls are exactly alike. They may share some characteristics in common, like siblings who share the same parents, but not even identical twins share everything. Calls, when they come, are specific. It is one thing to resolve to love people in general, but it is a whole lot harder to resolve to be nicer to a nasty coworker or a difficult relative. The specificity gives a call shape and substance.

So it is important to know who it is that is called. It is important to know that the main character of this story is not only a man named Jonah, but a specific Jonah, a product of a specific time, place, and set of parents. Only then do we have any hope of understanding our calls when they come—and come they do, welcome or not.

<<

[DH] *The word of the* LORD *came to Jonah . . .*
Go immediately to Nineveh. There could hardly have been a more unwelcome summons. To Jews like Jonah, Nineveh was notorious. The people there worshipped other gods, and a messenger from the Lord was unlikely to get a favorable reception. At best, Jonah could expect to get laughed at. At worst, he would be facing danger, and for what purpose? No one could seriously expect the Ninevites to respond to his message.

Nineveh was known not simply as a pagan city, but as a city of violence. The people of Nineveh were considered to be without pity or concern for others. Not only would Jonah have no wish to go there with a message for them, but he would want to stay as far from there as possible.

If it was dangerous to go even under neutral conditions, what kind of response could Jonah expect to the message that he was instructed to proclaim? He was called to enter this strange and hostile city, a city that even the Lord considered particularly wicked, and announce that God was about to destroy it. Have bearers of bad news ever fared well?

Finally, Jonah is given no time to prepare. He has no time to figure out if there might be a safe way to fulfill his call. There is no time for planning. He is to go *immediately.*

At times, that is how calls come to us as well: full of urgency, demanding an immediate response. And how might we respond? We hope, with "Here I am," like Samuel in the temple, like Isaiah in response to his vision, like Mary to the announcement that she would bear a son.[7]

But how do we in fact respond? Sometimes by dragging our feet and demanding more information. Sometimes by asking for authentication: like Abraham or Gideon, we demand a sign.[8] Or perhaps, like Ahaz, by refusing to ask for a sign, preferring not to be convinced of the reality of the call.[9] These are all wonderful ways to avoid responding, while still pretending (perhaps even to ourselves) that we are faithful.

Sometimes we demur, deciding that the call is impossible or that we are not qualified. Remember Moses who denied having the necessary eloquence?[10] And Jeremiah protesting that he was too young?[11] If the call seems impossible, it is much easier to pretend that we must be mistaken.

Jonah does none of these things. He does not demand authentication, for there are times when a call is so clear that we can have no doubts. He does not deny that he is at least minimally competent to carry it out. Presumably he could travel to Nineveh and deliver the message. He has no easy out.

Yet it is impossible for him to conceive of carrying out the call, not because it is impossible for him to perform physically, but because it goes against everything that he believes. Caught between the unequivocal demands of God and the violation of his sense of righteousness, he does the only thing that he believes a reasonable person could do. He turns tail and runs.

First Jonah goes to Joppa. Joppa was a thriving port city, the gateway to many places, many adventures. It would have been full of people from many places and goods from around the known world. Besides being in the opposite direction of Nineveh (a good thing in Jonah's eyes), it would be a wonderful place to get lost. In the midst of the busyness of Joppa, Jonah could hide.

Busyness is perhaps one of the best ways to hide. God's voice, when it comes, is often fairly quiet. It takes little noise to cover it up. By rarely being alone, rarely quiet enough to hear God's small voice, we deliberately avoid listening for God's call. Unable to hear God's demands, we embrace the louder but far less onerous demands on our lives.

And so we find ourselves on the way to Joppa, a familiar destination, for it's there we're caught up in the familiar, reliable, safe bustle and self-importance of our lives. In Joppa, we can drown out God's voice. In Joppa, we can ignore the command to go to Nineveh.

How often we fantasize about a quieter life, a more contemplative life, where we could be attentive to the still, small voice that calls to us so deeply. Like Jonah, however, when we are confronted with that call, we are tempted to flee into ever more busyness. "I just can't do it," we may say, shaking our heads in mock regret. "There's just no time, or no money," we may say, dismissing the call as some romantic but unattainable dream. "It's impossible," we may say in exasperation. "I don't have a minute to myself." As if to prove our point, we will plunge ourselves ever more deeply into the things that occupy us—and what better place to do that than in Joppa. It is amazing, as I look back upon such times, what I find. Suddenly projects that I have been putting off for years need to be done immediately. Things that I have completely forgotten about are suddenly remembered. New ideas demand my urgent attention. Crises manifest. It is amazing how productive and creative I become in Joppa!

Even these attempts to avoid the call, however, may not be enough. In spite of our efforts to banish them and to shut out the still, small voice with the cacophony of our lives, we may still be troubled by the call echoing quietly underneath. It is difficult to arrange our lives so that we are never alone. Even in the noisiest of lives, some quiet will creep in upon us. Even with televisions blaring, and children shouting, and cars honking, there will come those moments when all falls silent. Even a few moments are enough for the voice that never stopped speaking to be heard.

Joppa was not sufficiently noisy for Jonah to drown out his call. The noise and busyness did not completely still the voice. A more drastic action was required. So it was that Jonah made a conscious decision to escape the call. He did something that was completely incompatible with it: he boarded a ship headed for Tarshish.

Joppa may have been the wrong direction, but Tarshish was as far away from Nineveh as Jonah could possibly imagine. There was no way to get from Tarshish to Nineveh. In Tarshish, he would finally be free from the call. In Tarshish, he could finally escape the presence of the Lord. (Finding that pursuing a doctorate in biochemistry did not prevent me from hearing God's call, I needed to escape to Tarshish. So, I enrolled in a correspondence course to learn to be a photographer.)

In sailing for Tarshish, Jonah was leaving everything that he had previously held dear. He was leaving his family, his hometown, and even his people. He was willing to do anything to avoid that call. Any place was better than Nineveh. To avoid Nineveh, he was even willing to leave behind his God.

Even in the midst of our busy lives, God still calls. Like Jonah, we may be able to avoid hearing the voice for a time. As I did with my call to ordained ministry, we may decide that we are too busy, too poor, too frazzled to take on that call, as if a call was something to be added to our to-do list, along with grocery shopping and picking up the dry cleaning.

Calls, however, will not be denied so easily. For a time, we can submerge them in busyness, but God waits for those moments when we are vulnerable. God waits for those times when, despite our best efforts, we are alone and quiet. God speaks to us through a variety of sources: sudden thoughts, dreams, and even the voices of others. As Jonah discovered, even busyness is not sufficient to keep us from hearing the call to Nineveh. To really ignore a call, more drastic action is required.

Jonah thought that he could flee the presence of God. In his time, it was accepted that certain gods controlled certain lands. All he needed to do was to leave God's sphere of influence, and he would be freed of the Lord's demands.

In our monotheistic awareness, we no longer limit God's presence to a particular place. Schooled as we are in the idea that God created the whole world, the thought of physically fleeing God seems ridiculous

We can't limit our fleeing to physical escape. Our fleeing is often much more creative: we take a job that prevents us from going to Nineveh; we take some action that we think will disqualify us. Fleeing, as Jonah would agree, is the only sensible thing to do in the face of a completely unreasonable demand. Maybe by fleeing, we imagine, we can avoid the presence of the Lord. Perhaps the god of another land might be more reasonable.

I don't know if I had a particular destination in mind. I had yet to find one that I thought would be sufficient. Before I met with Martha I had considered several possibilities for flight—remaining in biochemistry, becoming a photographer, or some yet unimagined possibility. I wasn't terribly picky. I was hoping that Martha would help me to find my Tarshish, the place that would make it impossible for me to follow the call that was troubling me. Perhaps, I would become a photographer after all. . . .

Chapter 4

Call on Your God!

Jonah 1:4–6

CONVINCED that he has finally escaped his fate, Jonah goes down below in the ship to take a well-deserved break. A person can be excused for being just a little tired after all that running from God, for God is reputed to be a very fast runner indeed. Now all was well, for Jonah has indeed outrun God. He is safe, on his way to Tarshish, well out of God's reach. He can finally relax. Or so he thinks.

But Jonah has a lesson to learn. It is not possible to out-run God, for God is everywhere. Jonah believes, as so many people of his time did too, that Yahweh is confined to the land of the people of Israel. He thinks that he has left the Lord's sphere of influence, and he is now safely in some other god's territory. Of course it is possible that this new god might place demands upon Jonah, but the demand that he go to Nineveh is unlikely to be repeated by another deity.

That the Lord is confined to Israel seems a rather peculiar thing for Jonah to think, considering the nature of his call. After all, he is to preach to Nineveh that Yahweh is going to destroy it. If God can make it to Nineveh, is Tarshish impossible? Still, hope springs eternal. Perhaps Jonah thinks the Lord's hegemony does not stretch so far in the other direction.

Jonah is soon to be disillusioned. His fleeing to Tarshish does not put him safely out of reach of Yahweh, as he had hoped. In fact, it puts both his life and the lives of the ship's crew in mortal danger. A terrifying storm arises, destroying any illusion of security. Despite all of the crew's work, they are steadily losing their battle with the sea. In a frantic attempt to stay afloat they throw the cargo overboard, but it is to no avail. Everyone cries out to his or her own god, in hopes that one of them will be heard and the ship will be saved.

Everyone except Jonah. Tired out by his running, Jonah sleeps through the initial furor. It is not until the captain notices his absence and goes to look for him that Jonah is confronted with the consequences of his actions. He is directly responsible for the disaster about to engulf the ship and the crew.

The captain does not yet know of Jonah's culpability, but he has no great sympathy for the exhausted passenger he has taken on. A great wind, a fierce storm, a ship about to break up, a crew desperate for something to save them, and a foreigner asleep: the combination infuriates the captain. "Get up," he yells. "What do you think you're doing?" A passenger might not be much help in manning the sails, but surely he should be doing something. Anyone can pray. Even if the captain does not hold out much hope for the prayers of this foreigner in the midst of their calamity, he is not about to allow any possibility to go unexplored. "Call on your god," he orders Jonah.

That is the last thing that Jonah really wants to do. He has been doing his best to escape God. Why would he voluntarily enter into a conversation with the Lord? I suspect that Jonah hopes that God has forgotten all about him. We do not know whether Jonah did pray, but probably not, for the storm worsens.

Looking back on my call to my own Nineveh, I do not actually remember praying about it much. Since I was trying to pretend that such a call did not exist, I suspect that I ignored the subject altogether in prayer. I went to church. I read the Daily Offices. I prayed for those I knew who needed prayers. I did not, however, pray about my call. It was not a conversation that I wanted to have with God, for like Jonah, I was afraid of what I might hear.

Although I did not physically sleep through the whole year and a half that I struggled with my call, I tried to keep an important part of my life on an unconscious level. I tried to let this crazy call slumber while I pursued other options. But after my encounter with Martha, I was no longer allowed the luxury of sleeping in the hold. Like the captain, she forced me awake, forced me to confront the consequences of my decision. Like the captain, she reminded me that I had a responsibility not only to myself but also to my community. Like the captain, she ordered me to pray.

We can come up with a lot of reasons not to pray, but I suspect that the most basic reason is that we are afraid of what we might hear. We are afraid of what we will be asked to do. We are afraid that we will lose control. We are afraid that we will be asked to do things that we do not want to do. I think at that point, I was most afraid of losing control. Everything that I had planned, everything that I had worked for was fading away. No longer would I be in charge of my own life, and I wasn't quite sure what God might have in mind.

Prayer is dangerous stuff. We do not invoke God's name without risk. To call upon God is to make ourselves vulnerable. Even if we risk losing our lives, that choice would be ours to make. To choose to open ourselves to God, though, is to give all choice to God. Jonah stubbornly refused to heed the God who demanded that he go to Nineveh, even as the storm surged all around. Sometimes, the storms of our lives seem a whole lot less scary than the unknown. Sometimes, the storms seem a whole lot less scary than God. "It is a fearful thing to fall into the hands of the living God."[12]

Chapter 5

Tell Us Why

Jonah 1:7–10

THE storm continues to rage. Nothing that the crew does makes any difference. They lighten their load. They pray to their gods. They use all of their skill. It seems only a matter of time until their ship will break up, and they will be cast into the stormy sea.

In times of crisis, humans have a need to assign blame, to find a scapegoat. So it is that the crew pauses their frantic activity to determine which of them has gotten the gods so incredibly angry.

There are many ways in which humans assign blame. Sometimes we pick on the stranger, the one who is different or alien to us. Sometimes we pick on the person who is clumsier, or not as smart, or is simply socially maladapted. Often we choose those whose behavior does not correspond to the prevailing social norms, as was the case with the Salem witch trials. Usually it is someone whom we fear at some level. The sailors in the story of Jonah choose a different and perhaps fairer way: they cast lots.

Casting lots may seem to us to be a chancy way to decide guilt and innocence. We may distrust chance, but in the time of Jonah, casting lots was one way in which groups listened for messages from the gods. Throughout the Bible, casting lots was used to determine God's will, and even for determining guilt and punishment, as in the case of Saul and Jonathan.

When Saul could no longer hear the voice of God leading him, he cast lots to determine whose guilt had caused God's silence. He swore that whoever was at fault would die, and he was prepared to carry out the threat, even when the lots indicated that the sinner was his son Jonathan.[13]

In that case, the lots were accurate. Jonathan had indeed sinned, although inadvertently, and the fate of the fighting forces depended upon some punishment for the one who had violated Saul's imprudent oath. Until that happened, God's voice would not be heard, and they would be as lost as the sailors in the boat with Jonah.

Surely this tale or others like it would have been in Jonah's mind as the crew began to cast lots, for although the crew may have been unaware of the sinner among them, Jonah has no such clear conscience. He knows that God had told him to go to Nineveh, and he knows that instead of doing that, he headed in the opposite direction. He has done everything in his power to avoid God's command. Even if he had hoped that he had fled far enough to avoid God's wrath, he surely has a sneaking suspicion that the storm might be related to his actions. If at all possible, however, he is not going to admit it to the crew.

How often do we wish to keep our sins concealed! We conceal them from others, and that is perhaps the easiest form of concealment. We also try to conceal them from ourselves, coming up with some justification for having done the opposite of what we know we should have done. Perhaps, deep down, we even hope that we can conceal them from God as well. Adam and Eve certainly hoped that they would be able to do this, when they tried to hide from God in the Garden of Eden after eating the forbidden fruit.[14]

Surely this would have been a good time for Jonah to open his mouth, to tell the others about his sin that was endangering their lives, but Jonah does not do that. He remains stubbornly silent, hoping that the throw of the dice would indeed be random this time. Maybe someone else's sin would be uncovered, and Jonah could continue to pose as a righteous man to the others, to himself, and to God.

Like Jonah, in my struggle against my call, I depended upon silence. I thought that if I said nothing, the call would go away. I thought that if I said nothing, no one would know. I thought that if I said nothing, my failings could not be revealed.

The problem is that there was someone else who knew what I was hiding in my heart. That someone could not be fooled by my silence and was determined that I would fulfill what I was called to do, even if it meant exposing me to others. So the gap between who I said I was and how I was behaving was revealed, without my ever saying a word. How could I claim to worship God and yet be doing everything in my power to avoid God's call?

Without his ever saying a word, Jonah is also exposed as a sinner, a man whose sins have so angered the Lord, that God makes a major storm appear, a storm that threatens not only Jonah but also anyone unlucky enough to be caught in his vicinity. The silence that Jonah has hoped would protect him is shattered. He is stripped bare of all pretense in front of the crew. He can no longer hide from them, himself, or God.

"Why?" the sailors implore Jonah. "What have you done?" In the midst of great calamity, human beings demand answers.

If they were going to die in the storm, they had the right to know why. Knowing finally who was responsible, they cry out for understanding. "Tell us why we are perishing!"

"Why?" we also cry out in times of great trouble and anguish. "What has caused this?" we want to know. "Why? Why? Why?"

"Tell us who you are," they demand of Jonah, and reluctantly he complies. He names his tribe; he is a Hebrew. He names his god: the Lord, the Creator who has power over earth and sea. In that naming, he identifies himself in a deeper way. Yes, he is Jonah, son of Amittai. But the crucial thing is that the One he worships, the One who he claims to follow is the Lord.

Who is it that we worship? That question has deeper significance than we may first believe. As Annie Dillard reminds us, the One that we worship is no powerless object, but a being of great power: "It is madness to wear ladies' straw hats and velvet hats to church; we should all be wearing crash helmets. Ushers should issue life preservers and signal flares; they should lash us to our pews. For the sleeping God may wake someday and take offense, or the waking God may draw us out to where we can never return."[15]

Who is it that we worship? To what or to whom do we assign ultimate worth and value? The answer to that question says more about who we really are than our names and our lineage.

Who was it that I worshipped, as I struggled to avoid God's call? Perhaps I worshipped the god of convenience, when I told God that it was too late, since I was on another path. Perhaps I worshipped the god of the status quo, when I tried to avoid having my life turned upside down by God's importunate demand. Most likely, I was worshipping the god of self-autonomy by deciding that I could choose which commands of God I would follow.

What God was Jonah worshipping? "I worship the LORD,"[16] he proclaims—but does he really? Does worshipping the Lord mean making haste to get as far away from God as possible, in hopes of evading the Lord's commands?

Perhaps the sailors catch some of Jonah's fear, for their fears increase with Jonah's response. This is not a god with whom they are on speaking terms. This is not a god with whom they already have a relationship. This is not some local god they might be able to outrun in their boat. If this is the god who made the sea and dry land, there is no place to run. Interestingly, the sailors, who have little knowledge of the Lord, come to understand this almost at the same time that Jonah does.

What can they do? They have no hope of convincing this strange but obviously extraordinarily powerful god to save them. They know nothing about either Jonah's sins or the preferred methods of propitiation. Their only hope is to drag the information out of the accursed and reluctant Jonah.

"What have you done? How have you angered your god?" they demand of Jonah, and Jonah, exposed, tells them that he is fleeing the presence of the Lord. Fleeing from God: it sounds good. We all tend to flee in the face of a threat that is bigger than we can handle. Scientists call this the fight or flight response. It is almost instinctual.

God has become a threat to Jonah—a threat to Jonah's comfortable life, a threat to Jonah's understanding of the way in which the world should work, but most of all a threat to Jonah's very existence. Following this call will disrupt his life, force him to interact with people he considers evil, and perhaps result in his death. God has become dangerous, a danger that Jonah cannot possibly fight, so flight seems his only option.

It is strange that those of us who claim to follow God can come to see the Lord as a threat. We speak the language of giving ourselves up to God. We talk about dedicating ourselves to God in worship and prayer: mind, heart, and soul. Yet, when push comes to shove, we often do not want to hear what God might have to say. I suspect that somewhere deep down, we are afraid that if we really listen, our lives will never be the same. Most of the time, we are happy with being "good enough Christians." There is no point in going overboard, we tell ourselves and others.

Sometimes God has other things in mind. Sometimes we have to jump ship. It is no wonder that we sometimes perceive God as a threat, for God indeed threatens everything that we hold dear.

Chapter 6

What Shall We Do?

Jonah 1:11–13

THE crew discovers why they were in danger of perishing, but there is nothing that they can do about it. They are about to drown because Jonah is fleeing from his call, his country, and his God.

If the world were a fair place, as deep down we believe that it should be, it would have only been Jonah who was punished for his misdeeds. His sin should not have affected the sailors, who had no knowledge of the Lord at all. Jonah's punishment should have been his and his alone. Why should everyone else suffer for his misdeeds?

Unfortunately, the effects of our refusal to follow God's call don't affect us alone. The effect of such a refusal can be far-reaching. We are not called simply for our own sakes. Indeed, most importantly, we are called for the sake of service to others. Running from our call will not only affect the good that God would otherwise work through us, but sometimes it even causes great harm to others, as the sailors can attest. Call has a communal nature as well as an individual one. As transformative as our calls are for us personally, they have a larger purpose.

Jonah's refusal to go to Nineveh affects not only himself and the sailors on the boat, but the people of that city as well. After all, his call is to deliver a message, a message of judgment on the city. Without Jonah's voice, the people of Nineveh will not have any warning of the destruction that lies in their future. Nineveh is a large city. In the words of the book of Jonah, there are more than 120,000 children there. All of these children, and all of the adults, will remain in peril if Jonah ends up in Tarshish rather than Nineveh.

Denying our own call has consequences as well. Our refusal might only affect a few, but without our cooperation in God's purposes other people will suffer. Those whom we were meant to serve will remain unserved, and that part of God's plan will fall short of its potential.

There are also consequences for those who share our journey if we do not follow our call. To deny our call is, at its heart, to deny who we really are. By denying our call, we refuse to be the person who we were created to be. To deny our call is to live a lie, and living a lie affects all those who come in contact with us. They may come to understand why they seem to be caught in an unending storm, or they may remain bewildered by its source. Either way, chaos is introduced into their world.

While I was struggling against my call, my life seemed chaotic, out of control. I was failing as a biochemist. I could find nothing to do with my life that seemed both feasible and worth the commitment. Most of all, I could not be honest with myself and others about what was really going on inside of me. It took some time before I realized that I was in a storm of my own creation. Instead of allowing myself to be carried along with the current of God's vision, I was fighting against it. As long as I set my face in the opposite direction, the storm continued unabated, affecting not only me but also my husband, those I worked with, my friends, and fellow parishioners of my church. My work continued to go badly, and I could not figure out any way to right it. Friends and church members tried to help, but could not find a way to reach me. My husband, Mike, tried to help but could not, since he did not know the real source of my problem. Everyone found themselves affected, but unable to help me out of the storm caused by my resistance.

Like Jonah, I did not immediately confess that I was the cause of the storm. It is easy to attribute the storms in our lives to outside forces. It is easy to say that we are merely victims. It takes a great deal of courage and honesty to admit that we are the source of the storm, and at that point in my life, courage was in short supply.

Like Jonah, I did not admit my culpability to myself or to anyone else until I was confronted by Martha with evidence that I was indeed the cause of the storm. It often takes something from outside of us to break through our denial. The casting of lots by Jonah's fellow travelers or a confrontation by others can sometimes shatter our comfortable illusions. We have to be disillusioned.

The word disillusionment carries negative connotations, but it simply means losing our illusions. Unless we are disillusioned, we remain caught in a fantasy world, unable to see the reality of the world around us. Disillusionment forces us to deal with the way that things are, not the way that we would have them be. Disillusionment forces us to see the truth.

"You will know the truth, and the truth will make you free," Jesus promises his disciples.[17] Following God, listening for the voice of Christ, frees us from our illusions so that we may live fully. Unfortunately most of the time, I do not really want to be that free. Often I prefer to hold on to at least some of my illusions. I would rather believe that I am in control of my life. I want to believe that I can protect my family and myself. It is infinitely more comforting to believe that God is my servant, not the other way around.

In that moment on the deck, with the crew standing around him and the lots pointing to him, Jonah is disillusioned. He had thought that he could refuse God's command, avoid God's presence, and control his own life. Buffeted by a storm on the deck of that ship, he is faced with the truth and set free, but it was a freedom that would look like chaos, danger, and ultimate destruction.

When the crew asks him, "What shall we do with you?" Jonah's fate is in his own hands. He can try to hold onto his life and in the process sacrifice the lives of the crew, or he can choose to accept the consequences of his disobedience, giving those whose lives are bound up with his a chance to go on living.

"How do we get this wild and dangerous sea to quiet down?" the crew demands of Jonah. "You're the source of the trouble. You admitted it. Now you must be the source of the solution as well. Tell us what to do."

Jonah, bowing to his fate, tells them to throw him overboard. Only when he is finally removed from the boat will they be safe. He is willing for them to sacrifice his life for the good of the crew. If he is willing for them to toss him overboard, however, he is not willing to simply jump. He refuses to take the decision into his own hands, instead forcing the crew to accept the responsibility for his sacrifice. Jonah remains passive in the face of the danger that his actions have caused. Jonah is no hero.

"Do what you must," he tells them. "I won't oppose you. I'll understand if you feel you have to sacrifice me." In so doing, he lays a heavy burden on the frightened crew. Jonah does not take the initiative to remedy the situation. Instead, he forces the crew to decide between his death and theirs, between murder and suicide. He keeps himself above the messy calculations of right and wrong.

As frightened and concerned for their lives as the crew is, however, they are reluctant to throw Jonah to his certain death. In spite of the fact that he is the cause of their peril, they cannot abandon him to the roaring sea. In that, they prove themselves more righteous than Jonah, who is quite willing for the whole crew to die for his sins.

Faced with what they consider to be an unthinkable alternative, the crew redoubles its efforts to bring the ship back to land; an effort that they must know will be futile. They row hard, but the strength of their muscles is nothing compared to the strength of the storm. In fact, the fury of the storm only increases. The danger grows, and they are forced to admit that they have run out of hope. Only two choices lay before them: the deaths of everyone or pitching Jonah into the sea, for Jonah is the cause of the storm. As long as Jonah is on board, the storm will continue its fury and all in Jonah's vicinity will feel its power.

But oddly enough, many people justify their continuing resistance to God's call by citing adverse effects upon family and those around them should they obey. It would be too disruptive. I can't move the children. It would leave us economically strapped. All the while, they ignore the storm already raging around them.

I struggled with my call for a year before I talked to my husband about it. For that year, he knew that there was something wrong, but not what. When I finally told him, I hoped that he would agree that following this call was impossible.

For a little while, it seemed that this strategy would work. Every time I brought up the idea, he changed the subject. That situation, however, did not last very long. Like the sailors in the story of Jonah, he was much quicker to get the point of the storm than I, or perhaps he was just more faithful. He was ready to go where the sailing was smoother, even if that meant being married to a priest. He did not push me out of the boat at that point, but I certainly deserved it.

Chapter 7

Lord, Forgive Us

Jonah 1:14–16

EVENTUALLY the crew concedes defeat. They are trapped in the storm that Jonah has, through his arrogance and disobedience, brought upon them, and all of their work cannot save them. To try to save Jonah as well as their own lives is impossible. A choice has to be made.

It is indeed a terrible choice: to all die together or to follow Jonah's advice and throw him overboard. It is to the crew's credit that that they tremble before the decision and try every way around it that they can. Such a choice should never be easy. Is it God's will that they throw Jonah overboard? It will never be completely clear to them. They make the decision in humility and faithfulness, but they make it not at all sure of the outcome. They make it, trusting that the God who seems to demand this act will not punish them for carrying it out.

What do we do in those times in our lives when there seem to be no good decisions to be made? What do we do when it seems that no matter what we choose, disaster is sure to follow? How do we decide? Do we leave a marriage when there seems to be no hope of reconciliation? Do we have major surgery, when the chance of success is not 100 percent? Do we leave a job that is difficult, when we do not have another? Do we sever a relationship that has become unhealthy? It is not always obvious and making a decision in such circumstances can be dangerous.

Sometimes, the appropriate response is to wait. We may not have the information that we need, and time may help us to clarify the choices. Time may even show us new choices beyond the limited ones we had first discerned. Far too often we think that we have to make a decision right now, when all we are called to do is to wait. When the Israelites were not ready to enter the Promised Land shortly after leaving Egypt, God sent them back out into the desert to wait and to prepare themselves. When the next opportunity came, they were ready to make the decision to accept what God had promised to them. The man at the side of the pool of Bethzatha had been waiting for thirty-eight years to be healed.[18] Not having what he needed—loved ones to lift him into the waters when they were troubled—he had to wait. Wait for the coming of Jesus. The timing of events in our lives is not always under our direct control.

Rushing ahead to make a decision before it is time can have disastrous results. I suspect that if the crew had not taken the time to try to find a way to save them all, including Jonah, they would have felt very differently about their decision, about themselves, and even about God. They would have forever second-guessed their decision, and the weight of the responsibility would have been much heavier on their shoulders.

But there comes a time when a decision has to be made, and refusing to make a decision is in itself tantamount to making one. There comes a time when the boat is about to be swamped and the end (literally or figuratively) is near. The crew came to that place, and they were forced to decide. Unfortunately, in those times we often have to make a decision without being sure that we are making the right one. We often have to make a decision without knowing the full consequences. We often have to make a decision, trusting not in our ability to get it right but in the mercy of God.

The crew had prayed. They had listened. They had sought advice. They had explored all of their options. The decision before them was one that they had hoped to avoid, but they could avoid it no longer. So they place themselves in the hands of God and threw Jonah over the side of the boat, as he had told them they would need to do.

Finally forced to do that thing that they most wanted to avoid, the sea becomes quiet and tranquil. The storm is over.

I fought against my call for a year and a half. I refused to consider the possibility, ruthlessly suppressing any hint. I worked hard to uncover other possible careers. I tried hard to convince myself that I was not really qualified to be a priest. I was not ready to acknowledge the possibility to myself or anyone else, and I thought that as long as I never mentioned it, it would go away. In that time a storm raged around me, affecting not only me but also those who shared the same boat. The more I tried to get out of making that decision, the rougher the seas became. Like Jonah I held onto that boat, with its precarious sense of safety, for dear life.

Eventually, I would come to the same decision that the crew did in the tale of Jonah. The only way to get out of the storm was to accept God's call.

I remember the moment when I finally made the decision to seek ordination. I was sitting at our dining room table with the storm raging all around me. I was rehearsing all of the reasons why I could not possibly accept such a call. I was rowing for shore with all of my might. All of my rowing, however, only seemed to make the storm rage more furiously.

Finally I accepted, as the crew in the story of Jonah did, that this was indeed a call from God that could not be avoided. If God was calling me, then as a Christian I needed to accept it, impossible though it seemed. With that acceptance the storm ceased, and I, who had been in the midst of a great storm for a year and a half, was now at peace. The sound and the fury vanished, and like the crew, I was left in awe and amazement.

Although I had not been sure when I made the decision that it was the right one, once made, I could no longer doubt it. The change was too sudden, too dramatic to be explained any other way. I was aware that in that moment, I was in the presence of God.

The crew offered sacrifice and made vows—their acknowledgment of God's presence. I prayed and gave thanks, no longer afraid of the decision that I had made, for I knew then that God was indeed with me. That assurance was needed, because in spite of that moment of peace, following the call would not always ensure "smooth sailing."

Chapter 8

Facing Death

Jonah 1:17a

DOWN over the side of the boat goes Jonah. Down, down he is drawn into the raging sea.

What is Jonah thinking in those seconds as he plunges into the watery depths? Gone is the boat. What little safety it held would have seemed great in comparison to the situation in which he now finds himself.

What awaits him? The raging sea, of course. He has no protection and nothing to buffer its furious and pounding energy. He is powerless, completely in its grip.

What awaits him? I am sure that Jonah assumes that what awaits him is death. Even with a boat, survival is not assured, as evidenced by the panic of the sailors. Without a boat, no one could possibly survive in that storm. Jonah believes that he is in the very last moments of his earthly life. In those last few seconds, he is preparing for his death, reviewing his life, trying to make sense of who he is, trying to see the order that weaves it all together and has brought him to this end.

Contemplating our own deaths does have an effect. As people prepare to die, they have a need to look back and to remember, but most of all to make peace with their lives, in all of their glory and their tragedy, their holiness and their sinfulness. As we die, we need to somehow embrace the totality of our lives.

Jonah doesn't have time for a lengthy life review between when he is thrown overboard and when he enters the sea, although the process may have begun earlier. Surely when Jonah told the sailors that they needed to throw him overboard, he could see what lay ahead. When it didn't happen immediately, however, he may have relaxed, deciding that he had had his sentence commuted at the last possible moment. He may have thought that his offer would not be accepted.

We don't know how much time Jonah had after the crew began to think the unthinkable. Perhaps they discuss it a second time after their frantic but futile attempt to row to shore—or maybe the captain, made strong by fear, simply picks Jonah up and tosses him over the side with no warning at all. In any case, Jonah's time for preparation is limited, a matter of minutes rather than weeks or months. In spite of the short time, however, Jonah presumably prepares for his own death, as we all must do when confronted by our own mortality.

For a while, all goes as Jonah expects. He hits the water with a loud crash and feels the waves closing over his head. As he continues to descend, the light grows dimmer and dimmer, until at last he is in complete darkness. The pressure around his body increases as the water above bears down upon him. With the darkness and pressure comes cold, robbing his body of its heat. Jonah readies himself for death, perhaps hoping that it will come quickly, but now knowing that his life is not in his hands. He is, however, about to learn that even death could not be embraced unless it is God's will, and it is obviously not God's will that he die in the raging seas. He will live, but on God's terms.

Living when we expect to die is both a tremendous relief and a shock. On my honeymoon in Bermuda, my husband and I rented a moped. As we were driving back to our hotel, a car in a great hurry decided to pass us on a blind curve. Unfortunately, there was someone coming from the opposite direction. The first car suddenly pulled back into our lane, and we were forced to swerve abruptly to miss it.

Being relatively inexperienced in riding a moped—especially one with two people on it—we overcompensated. For what seemed like a very long time, we swayed back and forth until the moped finally fell over. I was thrown off in such a way that I fell facing the car behind us, which was hurtling toward us and our moped at great speed. I closed my eyes as I heard it crush the moped, fully expecting to die.

When I next opened my eyes, I was shocked to find that I was still alive. The car had run over the moped, but somehow had missed both my husband and me. Having anticipated my coming death, I was dazed, unsure of what to do next. I was soon helped up by those who had stopped to lend a hand. An ambulance was called, and we were taken to the hospital where we had the dirt and asphalt scrubbed out of the places where we had once had skin.

There was no lasting damage to me from that accident beyond a few not very noticeable scars, but I had changed. Having stared death in the face, I came to feel that my life was a gift, to be used for some purpose. For what purpose, I did not know, but I suspect that it was no coincidence that the idea of a call to the ordained ministry arose about a year and a half later. That gift of life imposed a sense of obligation. An obligation I eventually accepted.

Although I returned, at least for a time, to life as I had known it, Jonah did not. He isn't thrown back on the ship by a giant wave. He isn't washed ashore. Instead, he is swallowed by a big fish. It sounds like some kind of bizarre joke, not something that anyone could possibly believe. If this is some huge cosmic joke engineered by God, however, then the joke is obviously on Jonah.

I doubt whether Jonah sees the humor in the situation. Jokes are never funny for the person who has become the butt of the joke. As ridiculous as his predicament had become, only someone watching from the sidelines could have seen its humorous elements. Only we who hear the story second hand can laugh.

Instead, Jonah can only see that he is caught in a situation in which he has absolutely no hope of rescuing himself. If he hopes for a quick and dignified death, that hope is demolished. He is caught between life and death, condemned to live a life that is not really a life. A life that might end at any moment. For three days and three nights, a time that must have seemed endless, Jonah waits to see what will come next, for waiting is all that he can do.

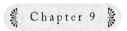

Chapter 9

A Very Large Fish

Jonah 1:17b

What was it like in the belly of the fish?

I picture Jonah in a large open area, the cavity that houses the organs, not residing in the stomach where he would surely have been digested in three days. Overhead, the ribs form the frame of his new dwelling, and covering their structure is a thick layer of muscle, fat, and skin. Perhaps a little light comes in through the gills as they filter the oxygen from the water, but not much. Or perhaps it is completely dark. It is, at best, a dark, damp prison. At worst, it is one where water poured in at regular intervals, threatening to drown Jonah. Most of all, it is a prison with no hope of escape.

There is no hope that Jonah can rescue himself. Neither is there any hope of rescue by the crew of the ship, for they would have given him up as lost when he never resurfaced. There is no hope of rescue by God, for it is God who provided the fish in the first place. Having no hope of rescue, then, Jonah waits.

Although I have never been swallowed by a fish, I do know what it is like to be in a dark place in life where I have no hope, and the only thing that I can do is to wait in the darkness, not knowing what lies ahead. If Jonah is anything like me, he doesn't simply sit down quietly to wait for something to happen. Like me, he probably tries everything in his power to get out of the terrifying, enveloping darkness. Only when I have tried everything in my power, only when I have exhausted my strength, do I quit my futile activity and accept the fact that I have no power to rescue myself.

Next come tears and screams of rage. Cries for help and tears of anger and frustration fill the darkness. Only when I have cried myself out, when my throat is raw with screaming and crying and when I have no energy even to bemoan my fate, only then do I accept that no one else can rescue me from the darkness either.

Then, and only then, when I have emptied myself of fear, of anger, of hope, and even of despair can I wait in silence for whatever comes next. Only then can I be at home in the darkness, not resisting, simply accepting. Only then can transformation occur.

Transformation is no easy task, as butterflies can attest. The change from caterpillar to butterfly requires a complete remaking of the body, dissolving the creature's old identity as caterpillar, before it can be reformed into the new. This process also occurs in a place of darkness.

Our own times of transformation may require us to enter a kind of cocoon, a place where God can dissolve our old identities and reform us into new creatures. Such radical transformation may seem impossible in the light of our everyday lives. Darkness may be God's way of easing us into the process of rebirth, for out of darkness, new life comes.

In the darkness of that time, confined within the belly of the whale, Jonah is transformed. He is transformed into the person he had claimed to be at the beginning of this story, one who worships the Lord. He is not made perfect in that time of darkness—as is made quite clear later in the story—but he is changed. He will become more fully the person God intends.

So it was that after three days, Jonah-the-disobedient-prophet becomes Jonah-the-worshipper-of-the-Lord. From the belly of the fish, he once again raises his voice in prayer. This time he does not raise his voice in fear or even petition, but in thanksgiving. What happened?

Chapter 10

Answer to Prayer?

Jonah 2:1–3

TRAPPED in the belly of the whale, having exhausted all of his options, and with no possible way of escape, Jonah prays. Surprising as it may seem, however, his prayer is not for deliverance, as we might expect. Instead he bursts into thanksgiving that his previous prayers have been heard.

Presumably, Jonah has already prayed at some point in this story. Possibly Jonah has prayed while on the ship. He very likely prayed as he was thrown over the side of the ship. It is hard to believe that he didn't pray as the water covered his head and he plunged deep into the sea. Presumably he did pray, but the answer to that prayer was surely unexpected and perhaps even unwelcome.

It seems highly unlikely that Jonah has asked for anything that has happened so far. I can't imagine that Jonah, on a ship that was about to sink, prayed to be thrown overboard, even if he admitted the necessity. I can't believe that Jonah, once thrown overboard, really prayed that he would plummet, like a stone, to the bottom of the sea. It is ridiculous to think that Jonah, about to drown, asked God to send a great big fish to swallow him. If Jonah had really prayed for things to happen just the way that they did, would it have taken him three days to start thanking God for answering his prayer?

How did God answer Jonah's prayer? Jonah, who has no desire to leave home and country, is commissioned to go to the very place that he most despised: Nineveh. When he attempts to head in the opposite direction, he finds that he can make no progress against the waves. In the midst of the storm, God does not soothe the waves in answer to prayer; they become even larger. Cast over the side, there is no convenient piece of driftwood for Jonah to grab. There is no friendly dolphin to take him ashore. He is not even granted a quick death, but instead finds himself in a living hell. After all of that, he thanks God for answering his prayer. If being trapped in the belly of a big fish is an answer to any prayer that Jonah might possibly have uttered, it is a mighty strange answer indeed.

We live with the illusion that we would be happy if only we could choose just how our lives would go. If God would only assure us that things would go just as we had planned, if God would only answer our prayers just as we wanted, we would be happy and content. If only we were in charge, all would be right with the world.

As circumstances have a way of reminding us, however, we are not in charge: God is. As surprising as it may seem, we are actually happier when we finally are driven to accept that we are human and God is God. Like children, we need someone who is more powerful than we are. We want someone to look out for us, not in the way that we desire, but in the way that we need. Jonah may not have had his prayers answered as he envisioned, but God is active, powerful, and present in Jonah's life. Relieved that God is indeed in control, Jonah bursts into a song of praise.

Like Jonah, my prayers have not always been answered in the way that I wanted. Although I had prayed during the time that I was struggling with my call to ordained ministry, my prayer was centered on finding some way to avoid the call. I wanted desperately to convince myself that it wasn't real. If only I could decide that I was not worthy. If only I could dismiss, once and for all, the idea that this was where I needed to go. I wanted to flee to my own Tarshish, and to do that I needed the storm to abate. In smooth waters, I could continue the journey that I had chosen.

In spite of all my prayers, strivings, and desires, however, I was not relieved of the burden of my call. In spite of my belief that I could only be happy if it went away, it never left me. In spite of the fact that I was sure what I wanted, it turned out that happiness came not from getting my own way, but in giving way to the one who was really in charge. Like Jonah, I only found peace when I at last allowed myself to brave the storm and be swallowed alive.

Indeed, I needed to give thanks. Through this process, I had learned in a vivid and dramatic way that I am not alone, even when I want to be alone. I learned that I don't always know what is best, even when I am convinced that I do. I learned that I am not in charge, no matter how desperately I wish that it were so. But, most of all, I learned that being in God's presence, accepting my limitations, and having a powerful and active God is indeed a cause for celebration.

From the bellies of our whales, we are all called to give thanks.

Chapter 11

Prayer in the Midst of Darkness

Jonah 2:4–7

TRAPPED in the belly of the big fish, surrounded by its bones and flesh, enveloped in inky blackness, Jonah is forced to come to terms with his situation, his life, and his God. Although thankful that he has not drowned, his situation is still critical. He is beyond rescue, beyond remedy, out of sight.

What do we do in these situations? What do we do when we are lost in the darkness? What do we do in the belly of the fish?

How do we pray when we feel utterly separated from God? How do we pray when there seems to be no hope? How do we pray in the midst of great darkness?

I often begin with cries of pain and desperate appeals for help. Later, my prayers typically turn to prayers of anger, as I rail against the one who seems to be deaf to my entreaties. Why have you done this to me, God? In those times, answers rarely come.

Finally, there comes a point when I am empty of all words, all feelings, and all energy. There comes a point when all that I can do is to sit and wait for whatever comes next. At this point, my only prayer is silence.

In those three days, Jonah presumably tried all possible ways to get out, even if that put him back in the same situation he had been in when he had been thrown overboard. He no doubt explored the fish's sides for any sign of weakness. He plotted and schemed. He tried again and again to do something, anything. He poured out all of his anger and frustration.

In those three days, Jonah has plenty of time to explore all of his options, and to find them all futile. There is time for him to try and try again, each failure weighing more heavily upon him. There is time enough for him to have been emptied—of anger, of frustration, and even of hope—until all that he can do is to sit in silence. Such times of silence are filled with great potential.

In that silence, Jonah is transformed. No longer is he the reluctant prophet fleeing an onerous calling. No longer is he the man asleep in the boat while others pray fervently to their gods. In that silence Jonah becomes what he has not previously been: a man of prayer.

It isn't a prayer of deliverance that pours from his mouth. No longer is his focus upon what he himself wants and needs. He tried that prayer and found it inadequate. In the darkness of the belly, he sees what he has not previously been able to see. His focus has turned from himself to God.

We might have expected that he would pray for deliverance. "Please, God, get me out of here!" Surely resolution of that crisis is a necessary first step. That isn't, however, what Jonah prays. In the belly of the fish, Jonah is aware of all that he had lost, and chief among the things that he has lost is a sense of God's presence. In the belly of the whale, he feels utterly separated from God. The man who desperately tried to run away from God is now confronted with the consequences of his actions. In a strange way, he gets what he wanted, and he is bereft. "I am driven away from your sight." he laments. "I will never again see the temple. I will never be able to worship you in the place where you dwell. I have lost something beyond value."

How often we think that we know what we truly desire. If only this particular thing would happen, then all will be well. If only I get this job, I will finally be happy. If only a family member straightens up, all of our problems will be solved. If only I could buy what my heart desires, I will be content. If only a certain person would love me as I love them, we could live happily ever after. If only. . . .

Our hearts are full of such longings. Some are stronger than others. Some are more important than others. All of these often conflicting longings war within us, seeking to be fulfilled. We are creatures full of desires.

As Jonah discovers, getting what we desire does not always make us happy. None of our desires can ever fill the empty place in our hearts, except for God. Without God, nothing else matters. Having learned this much, Jonah grieves his loss, a loss far greater than the loss of his freedom or even the loss of his life.

What do we do in times of grief? What do we do when we have lost someone whom we have loved? We tell the stories of the ways in which our lives and theirs intertwined. We tell the stories over and over again. That is what Jonah does as well. He recites the story of the last time that he felt the hand of God in his life.

As he had been drowning, at the moment when the seaweed was pulling him to the bottom of the ocean and his life was ebbing away, the One from whom he was running intervened. Through the hand of God, the fish swallows him. As strange as that is, and as problematical as his presence in the fish now is, Jonah has cause to be thankful, for God is powerfully present.

In the darkness of the fish's belly, Jonah is transformed. He can now see God at work in his life in new and peculiar ways. He can give thanks, even in the impossible situation in which he now finds himself. He has come through the darkness, and is now ready to reenter life. With this change in Jonah, another change happens. The fish, which had been keeping him imprisoned, now vomits him up onto dry land.

It is a new birth for Jonah, and as inelegant as births are. His life ends when he is thrown overboard, but through the love and grace of God, he is given new life.

Chapter 12

Go to Nineveh (Again!)

Jonah 3:1–3a

SPIT up on dry land, Jonah once again hears the voice of God. He is given no opportunity to recover from his three-day-long ordeal in the belly of a fish before the call comes once again. Already too much time has been wasted in his flight from Nineveh. "Get up," God tells Jonah. "You have work to do."

After being thrown overboard and almost drowned, after being swallowed by a fish and residing in its guts for three days, Jonah is a different person. The voice from heaven, however, has not changed: the message is the same one that he heard while still in his own land. "Go to Nineveh," God commands, and this time Jonah heads in the right direction.

Heading in the direction that God calls him, things go a whole lot better. There are no storms. Jonah is not thrown overboard. No fish make their appearance to swallow him whole. He arrives without further incident. Though perhaps not yet reconciled to the thought of preaching to the Ninevites, Jonah is at least obedient. He goes according to the word of the Lord, and although God really prefers enthusiastic agreement, God is realistic enough to simply accept reluctant obedience.

What keeps Jonah moving forward to Nineveh? I suspect that it isn't the promise of proclaiming God's word to the inhabitants. That was not sufficient impetus originally. If anything keeps Jonah moving, it is probably the memory of the struggle that has brought him to this place: an implacable storm, a near drowning, and a hungry fish.

There were many times during the long and sometimes trying process toward ordination when I wanted to back out and to return to my home and previous existence. Sometimes, following that call seemed too complicated, too messy, and too difficult. Having decided that I was called, I was ready to start for Nineveh. But I was forbidden from starting that journey until I first got some kind of degree in biochemistry. God might accept as a priest someone who failed biochemistry, but the church had higher standards. What kept me going in spite of all that? It was only the memory of the struggle through which I had already traveled. Whatever else I might think, I could no longer doubt that I was doing what I was called to do. My experiences, like those of Jonah, instilled obedience, even if at times that obedience was reluctant.

At times, the assurance that I did indeed have a call was a great source of strength. I found that those of my classmates who had a reasonably smooth path in the beginning of the ordination process often hit a time during seminary when they questioned their call. That was less common among those of us who had already spent some time in the belly of the fish. The process was like an inoculation. The needed antibodies had already been formed, and we were protected to some extent against future occurrences. We did not consider running away, because we already knew the consequences of such flight.

Like Jonah, we set our faces toward Nineveh and the tasks ahead of us. If we were called to Nineveh, we would go to Nineveh. Perhaps, that initial struggle was indeed an important part of the sense of call. I suspect that any call may require a time of trial, a refining by fire. In that process, we are strengthened for the difficult work that we are given to do.

Becky had wanted to be a teacher, and she had begun college, working on that goal. While in college, she fell in love. Marriage and motherhood put that call on hold for a while, but it did not banish the call. She knew that one day, she would become a teacher. In spite of family opposition and a lack of money, she persevered. At times, it did not look like she would make it, but always the call beckoned her. After graduation, when there were no jobs in the area, she had to move a long way to answer that call, all the way to Nineveh.

A call requires a willingness to sacrifice. Although different people are asked to sacrifice different things, a real call requires sacrifice. At the very least, a call requires us to sacrifice other possibilities for our lives and ministries. To marry one person requires us to give up the chance of meeting and marrying others. To be a parent requires us to give up much in time, money, and even sleep. To dedicate ourselves to one career requires us to sacrifice the possibility of other positions. To accept a call means to limit our options in important ways.

After being spit up by the big fish, Jonah's options are limited, limited enough so that he sees only one real choice. He sets out for Nineveh in obedience to God's word. In doing that, he leaves behind his family, his country, and even his old self. The person who had felt free to ignore God's commands, the person who had thought that he could flee when God got too pushy, the person who had believed that he was in control of his life, died in the process. This new Jonah, by no means perfect as we shall see, is quite different in many ways.

So it was for me, as I set out for seminary. I had been transformed. Although I can ultimately still ignore God's commands (at least for awhile), I no longer really believe that I can avoid God's call. I have found that I cannot flee far enough to outrun God. I have learned (although I still forget on occasion) that I am not in control: God is.

A call may come in many different ways. It can come quietly or in spectacular ways. It can come in an instant or develop over long periods of time. In each case, however, God breaks into our world, claiming us and reminding us that we were created to do God's will. Only in responding to our call will we ever find the peace and wholeness for which we yearn.

I suspect that as much as he had dreaded going to Nineveh, Jonah is glad to finally have the issue resolved. I know that it was with that mixture of excitement, relief, and apprehension that I began my journey to ordination

Chapter 13

Woe to Nineveh!

Jonah 3:3b–4

SO it was that Jonah arrives at last in Nineveh, that great and powerful city, the home of his enemies, the place that he has tried so hard to avoid.

It is obvious that preaching to a city of that size would be no small task. Pardon the pun, but Jonah is given a whale of a task. Even just walking across Nineveh takes three days—not counting the time it takes Jonah to stop, gather a crowd, and proclaim his message.

The message that he is to proclaim to the people of Nineveh is clear. In forty days, that city will be destroyed. If Jonah fears for his life in delivering what was bound to be an unpopular message, he is more afraid of what might happen should he fail. Although determined at last to fulfill his unwelcome commission, I cannot imagine that Jonah put anything more into the task than is absolutely necessary.

I imagine Jonah hurrying through the streets until he finds a gathering place, then gasping out his message quickly and sprinting onward before the crowd has time to attack him. Perhaps he hopes that they might not really pay attention to him. Perhaps his message will be lost in the noise of the crowds. Or perhaps the people of Nineveh will decide that he is a madman, and dismiss him altogether. If they do not pay attention to him, he will probably escape harm. So it is that Jonah journeys further and further into the city he has tried so hard to avoid.

Although Jonah might have feared for his life, I do not think that the content of the message he has to deliver is particularly unwelcome to him. He has no love for the people of Nineveh, and I doubt if he cares whether the city perishes. Perhaps, he hopes that it will indeed come true. That is consistent with his actions later in the story, when he sits in his front row seat, waiting for destruction to rain down upon them.

In any case, Jonah is obedient to his call. He travels through the city for many days. He proclaims the message of judgment he has been given. His fears, however, are unfounded. He is not accosted. He is not subjected to violence because of his message. He is not prevented from completing his commission. In fact, he has "success" far beyond anything that he could have imagined.

That is the strange thing about a call from God. Even when we are excited about it, it often does not go the way we have pictured in our minds. We build up a wall of excuses and fears that prevent us from doing what we know, deep in our hearts, that God is calling us to do. We focus upon all of the things that prevent us from accomplishing the task. We rehearse all of the reasons that such a call is impossible.

With God, however, all things are possible, as Jonah finds out. His fears are baseless. He, a person of a despised race and country, is allowed to move freely. He tells the people of Nineveh things that no person would ever want to hear. He penetrates their city, filling it with cries of God's coming vengeance, and no one accosts him. What seems to be impossible is indeed possible.

God does not call us to impossible tasks. If it is truly a call from God, then it is possible, no matter how unlikely it seems. Somehow, in some way, we will have the strength and resources that we need. When Teresa of Avila was asked how she planned to start a monastery with her small number of *ducats*, she replied that with Teresa and the *ducats*, it was impossible. With God, however, all was possible. She started not only one monastery, but seventeen. When we are following God, we are not in it alone, and all of the power and resources of God are present.

It may not be obvious how God plans to accomplish the task. It may look as if God is leading us into a blind alley, with no way to exit. Like the Israelites, we may find ourselves caught between the Pharaoh's army and the Red Sea with nowhere to go.[19] We may feel trapped and helpless, but we are not in this alone. God will provide what is necessary, if we only step out in faith and trust.

I wonder when Jonah realized that his fears were baseless. I wonder how long it took before Jonah realized that this task was indeed possible. I wonder how long it took Jonah to stop fearing for his life as he wandered through Nineveh preaching.

Probably quite a while. At least in my own life, I have trouble believing that the impossible is really possible. I keep waiting for the other shoe to drop. I keep expecting to be proven right. It is usually a long time before I am able to trust that God really knows what God is doing. I am much more comfortable when things go as I expect them to. After all, I know what I am doing, and I am not always certain that God does!

Yet, time and time again, God reminds me that God really does know. In fact, God is a whole lot better at ordering the world than I am. I may have an idea of the *potential* problems of a course of action, but God knows what they really are. I may have plans for how to deal with expected crises, but God can manage them much more effectively than I. I may think that only certain things are possible, but with God many of my impossibles are indeed possible.

Preaching destruction to a large city of enemies without losing one's head may seem impossible, but as Jonah finds out, when the plan is God's, it's not difficult at all. The problem is not with the preaching or with a negative response by the people. The problem comes from something that Jonah could not have imagined. What do you do when your enemies heed your warnings? That would indeed turn out to be a problem for Jonah, a bigger problem than if they had just thrown him out of the city unheard.

Chapter 14

The Conversion of Nineveh

Jonah 3:3–9

JONAH has reason to worry about the response to his message: he is a foreigner, a member of an enemy nation, and he is telling them they are going to be destroyed. Violence is not out of the question. Instead, he makes his way, unmolested, a third of the way across the city.

At best Jonah might have imagined that he would be the object of derision for his message. The populace of this great and powerful city had nothing to fear from the smaller, weaker Israel. In a time when the power of a god was measured by the power of its people, it is hard to imagine that the Ninevites would have felt threatened by a prophecy of this lesser deity. Amusement or scorn would not have been unexpected. "Just who does he think that he is!"

The people of Nineveh, however, are not laughing.

Instead of violence, instead of scorn, they listen seriously to his cries of doom and gloom. They listen, and even more surprisingly, they respond in a completely unexpected way. They see in Jonah's preaching a call to a new way of life. They are converted by his message, repenting of their misdeeds. The words of this reluctant prophet are enough to reach the whole of the city.

Everyone listens, and they all throw themselves heart and soul into expressing their repentance. A fast is proclaimed that touches not only the people of Nineveh but the herds and the flocks as well. Not only will the human inhabitants of Nineveh cry out to the Lord, but the animals in their distress will cry to heaven as well. The king commands the people to dress in sackcloth, and even the animals are draped. All Nineveh will be united in a great show of public repentance.

It is an amazing sight: the king, dressed in sackcloth and covered with ashes, is in the midst of a people dressed likewise. The lamentations of the people are mixed with the bleats of sheep and goats and the lowing of cattle.

What an amazing response to the reluctant prophet's words. But, of course, they aren't really Jonah's words at all. Given a choice, he would have said nothing to the people of Nineveh. Given a choice, he would have gone on his way rejoicing, while the unprepared inhabitants perished for their wickedness. The words that Jonah proclaims are not really Jonah's words, they are the word of the Lord, and their power transforms the people of Nineveh.

The people of that city do not argue about the justness of the sentence that is imposed upon them. They acknowledge the violence that is a part of their lives. They admit that there is evil in their city. They accept that the fierce anger of the Lord is indeed justified.

Knowing that there is no hope for them in the court of justice, they throw themselves on the mercy of the Lord. Maybe, just maybe, if they show their contrition, God will be appeased. Maybe, just maybe, if they turn to a new way of life, the Lord will allow them to live. Maybe, just maybe, there is some reason to hope.

Throwing themselves upon the mercy of God, the Ninevites unknowingly follow a long-standing pattern in Jewish tradition. Time and time again, the anger of the Lord burned hot against the Israelites for their misdeeds. Time and time again, God had been poised on the brink of destruction. Time and time again, at the last minute, the Lord relented. When the world got too evil, God was ready to wash it all away in a flood.[20] When the people made the golden calf in the desert, God was ready to smite them.[21] In spite of God's great anger, however, the Lord is a God of mercy, not of vengeance. Over and over again the Hebrew scriptures rejoiced in the loving kindness of God.

The people of Nineveh are unlikely to know the history of this God, whose people lived far away. Even if there were people in the city who had heard of the ways in which the Lord had forgiven the people of Israel over and over again, why should they expect the Lord to look favorably upon them? They are enemies of the Israelites, known for their violence and evil ways. Why would the God of the Hebrews save them?

In spite of this, they hope against hope. They hope, having no other choice—for to live without hope is a fate worse than death. "And who knows?" asks the king. "Perhaps the unthinkable will indeed happen. Maybe there is a chance."

What will be the response when we, like Jonah, finally decide to live out our calls? We may think that we know what will happen. We may believe that they are fools' errands doomed to fail. We may worry about the consequences for us and for those we love, but we do not really know, any more than Jonah knew. The results may be beyond what we can imagine.

Who knows what will happen in response to God's urging? Only God really knows for sure.

Chapter 15

Changing God's Mind

Jonah 3:10

THEIR change of heart was impressive, and the people of Nineveh go all out to show their willingness to change their ways. The whole city is called to mourning for their sins. Even the animals, presumably not responsible for the sins of Nineveh, are affected. All cry out in distress.

What prophet could have hoped for anything more? The people's response shows a great deal of desperation. I suspect that if the king had been able to think of anything else to do, he would have ordered it.

Through the actions of the people of Nineveh, the Lord is shown to be in control of the whole world, not just the land of the Israelites. The lesson that Jonah has to learn the hard way in the belly of the fish, the people of Nineveh grasp just by hearing his message of condemnation. Impressive.

Apparently, the Lord thinks so as well. Gratified by the lengths to which the Ninevites go to make amends, the Lord decides not to visit vengeance upon them. Although punishment would have been justified, God rejoices that such drastic action proves unnecessary. Instead of wiping them out (a tactic proven less than effective in the flood)[22], God gives them a chance to try again. Perhaps they really have seen the light, or at least have had enough of a scare to make them decide to shape up.

That raises an interesting question. Has God really been expecting them to turn over a new leaf after Jonah's preaching? Maybe not, for according to the Bible, God changes God's mind.

The portrait of God in the Old Testament is not like the unchanging, passionless god pictured by the Greek and Roman philosophers. The God of Israel is one who gets angry—and one who responds in love. The God of Israel is one who destroys, and one who protects. The God of Israel is one who can sometimes have a change of mind and heart. In God's willingness to change God's mind, the contrast between God and Jonah is even more evident: Jonah is one who changes his mind only when forced to do it.

Remember, Jonah originally had no intention of preaching to the people of Nineveh. When he got the call to go, he went to extreme lengths to make sure that he was headed as far from Nineveh as possible. He was willing to leave behind his family and people, simply so that he did not have to go to Nineveh. His mind was made up, and that was that.

Even caught on a ship in the middle of the storm, with his life and the lives of the whole crew in danger, Jonah refused to change. He refused to pray to God, for if he did, he would acknowledge the Lord's power over his life. To acknowledge the Lord's power over his life would mean giving in to God's command for him to go to Nineveh. Even when forced to choose between losing his life and changing his mind, he chose the former. As he was thrown overboard and the waters closed over his head, he could at least console himself with the thought that he never gave in: he did not go to Nineveh.

Little did Jonah know that God was more interested in making sure that he got to Nineveh than in punishing him for his disobedience. Considering all of that, he shouldn't have been surprised by the Lord's reaction to the people of Nineveh. The Lord had a long history of making sure that people went where they were supposed to go, and did what they were supposed to do.

If Jonah thought that dying would save him from going to Nineveh, he was sorely mistaken. Not only his life, but also his death was in the hands of the Lord. The purpose of the storm was not to take his life (as he had assumed), but to change his mind. The fury of the storm was absolutely necessary, for Jonah did not change his mind easily. Only when spit up on land and told again to go to Nineveh, only when he had finally acknowledged the complete futility of doing anything else, did Jonah finally change his mind.

Jonah would have assumed then that the destruction of Nineveh was a high priority for the Lord. After all, look how hard God had worked to get Jonah to Nineveh to preach his message of doom and gloom. There were no ifs, ands, or buts in that message. "Forty days and you are dead. You have had your last chance. It's all over."

In spite of the uncompromising message, however, God's mind is changed. A few ashes, some empty bellies, and the awful caterwauling of sheep and cows bellowing for lack of food and water is enough to change the whole plan. Hasn't the Lord ever heard of deathbed confessions? Everyone knows that they are not to be trusted. The Lord should be more like Jonah. You won't catch Jonah changing his mind simply because the Ninevites promised to do better!

Jonah, unbending and unchanging, comes across as the changeable one. He is thankful that God is merciful when it concerns him, but resents it in the case of the Ninevites. In spite of the Lord's apparent change of mind in the case of the destruction of Nineveh, God is consistently concerned not with punishment but with transformation.

Throughout the book, the Lord is shown as a God of forgiveness. Whether the one needing forgiveness is a disobedient prophet or a wicked city, the Lord is merciful. Both Jonah and the city of Nineveh are saved from their just punishments. In both cases, the Lord grants them life, even though they deserve death.

Throughout the book, the Lord is interested in transformation. Jonah is transformed from a disobedient worshipper into a reluctant prophet. Nineveh is transformed from an evil, violent place into a city full of repentance and promises of amendment of life.

In fact, if the Lord had gone through with the planned destruction and had refused to change God's mind, then we would have seen a God whose purposes wavered. Surely a God who blew up a storm and provided a great fish in order to affect the transformation (however reluctant and partial) of one person would be delighted by the much more thorough conversion of a whole city.

It's not that God is wishy-washy, but that God is willing to give up what Jonah thought that God wants (the destruction of Nineveh) in order to accomplish what God really wants (the conversion of the city). Jonah, unwilling to see anything but a simple destruction or preservation decision, is not happy.

As I look back on my life, there have been many times when it seemed to me that God was capricious and changeable. There have been times when I thought that I understood what God wanted, only to have everything turned upside down.

I certainly thought that I was following God's will as I pursued a degree in science. To have it all brushed aside a few years into that process was maddening and frustrating. Why didn't God make up God's mind!

Perhaps God had, and like Jonah I did not see the underlying unity of God's actions. The work of transformation is often quite hidden, and although we can sometimes glimpse the next step, the end is always beyond our sight.

Chapter 16

Let Me Die

Jonah 4:1–3

THINGS were definitely not going the way that Jonah had envisioned them.

He never wanted to come to Nineveh at all. He considers this mission to the people of Nineveh a waste of his time and energy. They are wicked, through and through, fully deserving of any thunderbolts that might come their way. With such people, the best thing is simply to stay far, far away.

So Jonah had slipped onto the boat headed for Tarshish. From that distance, they would leave him alone, and he would do likewise. He would not even have to think about Nineveh. In Tarshish, Jonah could put them far from his mind.

God, however, insisted that Jonah go to Nineveh to tell them of their coming destruction. In fact, God refused to take no for an answer, going so far as to conjure up violent storms and big fish, so that Jonah would be forced to tell the people of Nineveh that God was just about to zap them.

Jonah traveled to Nineveh and told the people that they would be destroyed, as God had instructed him to do. He risked life and limb to preach that unpopular message. His only consolation through all of this was that he would see those wicked, wicked people get exactly what was coming to them.

Then what do you think that God goes and does? God decides to spare Nineveh, just because they get their act together at the eleventh hour. How could God have been taken in by all the melodrama, all the weeping and gnashing of teeth, all the lowing of cattle?

Of course, Jonah knows that such a reprieve is a possibility. God is not to be trusted to carry out sentences of judgment. God has this bad habit of talking tough, but then going soft at the crucial moment. Not only does that make God look wishy-washy, but it also makes a laughingstock out of Jonah, who has proclaimed that God is going to get the people of Nineveh.

All of this makes Jonah very mad. "All right, God," Jonah yells to heaven. "Just what do you think you are doing? Why did you get me all the way out here if you knew that you had no intention of destroying Nineveh? Did you do this just to make me look bad, because if you did, the joke is over! I'm tired of being the butt of your jokes. I'm tired of being jerked around. If you're going to play cat and mouse, just finish me off. There's no reason for me to continue to live." Robbed of any possible recourse for God's breach of wrath and judgment, Jonah does what any reasonable adult would do: he sulks. God is not playing fair.

Often, God has other ideas than we do. In fact, in my experience, God delights in turning upside down all thoughts that we might have about our call, and about how they are to be fulfilled. Like Jonah, we may be quite sure what it is that we are called to do (such as preach destruction), only to find out that something else happens altogether. Like Jonah, we may be angered by what we believe is God's treachery, or sometimes depressed by our inability to make things work out the way that they are supposed to.

During the time that I was struggling with my call to ordained ministry, I was in the midst of a doctorate program in biochemistry. I had gotten to the point where I was at least conceding that maybe someday I would need to answer a different call. First, however, I had to finish what I had started.

Shortly after that, I almost flunked out of the graduate program. Unfortunately, the class that I failed was only offered once a year, so I would have to wait a whole year to take it again.

I had done my best, but I had great difficulty in wrapping my mind around the material. I had worked and studied hard, but all of that effort produced little enlightenment. Because of that, I had no real confidence in my ability to do better the next time. For the first time in my academic career, my best effort was not enough. All that I had planned, all that I had counted upon, was turning to ashes. It wasn't simply that I had failed a class, but that I was a failure. Like Jonah, I had seen all that I had worked so hard to accomplish crumble before me.

I could not even claim, like Jonah, that it was all God's fault that I was in this mess. After all, I had not felt pushed into biochemistry. I had done it because I enjoyed it, and it was what I wanted to do. There was no one to blame except myself. My response was not anger at God, but anger at myself—and ultimately depression.

Seeing myself as a failure, I did not believe that I could have a call to ordained ministry. Surely God would want the best people for priests, not a failure like me. Convinced that I knew how God thought and felt (in fact, thoroughly convinced that God thought and felt the same way that I did), I rejected my call as impossible: God could not possibly want me.

It was a long and difficult year. Like Jonah, I felt cut off from everything else. I felt far from family and friends. I felt that my call (both to science and the priesthood) had proven false. I had failed to accomplish what I had set out to do. Like Jonah, I felt angry enough to die.

But, like Jonah, I didn't. I lived to see another reality emerge, one that I could never have imagined. Like Jonah, I was being taught some new and difficult lessons about God and about myself. Like Jonah, I was being taught that God doesn't always think the way that I do. I learned that God might have a completely different outcome planned, even when I thought I was doing what I was "supposed" to do.

Chapter 17

Jonah's Pout

Jonah 4:4–6

"I AM angry enough to die," Jonah proclaims. He is angry at the way things have turned out, and even more to the point, angry with God. He feels used, abused, and manipulated in order to force him to pronounce doom upon Nineveh. He had not wanted to be the prophet of doom, but God insisted. Now, though, there is no destruction. He has been made a laughingstock.

As far as Jonah is concerned, God should end his life right then, but God does not choose to end his life. Instead of being zapped with a lightning bolt for his temerity in questioning the divine actions, God deals Jonah a rebuke, calling into question whether Jonah's anger is really justified. Jonah does not even consider the question worthy of a reply. Of course it is justified, Jonah thinks.

Deprived of his opportunity to make a melodramatic exit, Jonah builds himself a shelter and waits to see what will happen. Perhaps God will change God's mind once again. With God, anything is possible. I doubt that Jonah really believes that God will destroy Nineveh, but what is a prophet to do? So he sits and waits and stews, and nurses his anger.

In that state, Jonah would have seen any discomfort as a further sign of God's unfairness. He should have been being rewarded for all that he had done. Instead, he was stuck sitting on the hill above the city, waiting for something that would probably never happen. At least God could have made Jonah comfortable in the meantime, but God doesn't even provide any shade. Jonah has to make his own to protect himself from the scorching noonday heat.

As Jonah sulks and nurses his grudge, he recites to himself all the ways in which he has been mistreated. Every once in a while, he insists that it would have been better to die. If only he had been in charge, things would have been done right!

How often we wish that we could order the world the way that we see fit. That is often at the bottom of our sulks and anger when things don't turn out the way that we envision. Unfortunately, what seems right to us is not always the way that God does things. Often when we see only one way to resolve a situation, God will come up with some other possibility. It would be all right if that other possibility was obviously better, but sometimes it seems a great deal worse. If only God would do things our way, we would be happy, and the world would be a much better place, or so we think.

God, however, doesn't do things our way. God doesn't always resolve situations as we would have done if we inhabited the heavenly throne. There may be occasions when we can admit that God actually did something better than we would have done—but such an insight is rarely immediately obvious. On the other hand, there are a whole lot of times when it seems obvious that God has screwed up.

Not being able to change God's mind, not having the power to force God to do things our way, and not being God, there is little that we can do other than accept our lack of control, or pout. Acceptance is difficult, as it requires some belief, some trust that God really does know how to fix the world better than we do. It requires us to admit that perhaps we don't always know the best way to resolve the world's problems. It requires us to admit that we are creatures, not the creator.

That is not easy for human beings. According to our biblical heritage, being willing to accept our role as limited humans was difficult from the beginning of human existence. Not content with the single rule governing the Garden of Eden, Adam and Eve preferred to take their fate in their hands. They wanted to be in charge. Unfortunately, insisting upon being in charge usually gets us into trouble. It got Adam and Eve kicked out of the Garden.[23]

Even if there were not serious consequences to our desire to usurp God's prerogatives, however, such behavior distorts our proper relationship with God and with others. We begin to show displeasure with others who do not recognize our exalted position. We become angry when we do not receive the proper deference. We get sulky and out-of-sorts when things do not go our way. Like Jonah, we may pout, and as long as we pout, we will be unable to see the new and exciting thing that God is doing.

All Jonah is able to see is that God is not doing what God has promised. Nineveh is still standing. The Ninevites are still making their appeal to heaven. The cattle are still bawling, complaining of their lack of food and water. The world spread before him is not one that he wished to be a part of, and the only way to leave is death.

Jonah cannot see the change taking place in the hearts of the Ninevites. He cannot see the greater miracle that God is working. He cannot see the new life that God is bringing forth. He is blind to God working in and through the situation. All Jonah can see is the death of what he had imagined.

How does God reach us when we, like Jonah, have retreated into pouting? How does God restore our sight, when we have been blinded to anything new that God might be doing? How does God convert our hearts? Sometimes, as the people of Nineveh knew and as Jonah would soon find out, it takes an intervention to restore sight. In Jonah's case, it would require a bush, a worm, and most of all, a sultry east wind.

Chapter 18

Jonah, the Bush, the Worm, and the Sultry East Wind

Jonah 4:6–8

SO God "appoints a bush,"—a curious turn of phrase. The choice of words makes it clear that this bush does not appear by mere chance, but as a part of a plan. The bush is not simply an object in the story, but has become a character in the drama.

Of course, we might be expected to see the hand of God in this bush that grows to such a stature that it could shade Jonah in one day. God's hand is also surely to be seen in its placement: it grows right beside the booth that Jonah has made. Even Jonah is aware that God is at work in its appearance.

I wonder what he thinks as the plant grows up? Maybe he thinks that this plant is his consolation prize. Maybe he considers it a veiled apology from God for the way that he has been treated. Maybe Jonah thinks that it is a bribe, to get him over his horrible mood. Maybe he considers it a signal that God is finally coming around to his way of thinking. Whatever the case, as a result of the bush, Jonah is in a better frame of mind, a little more content and at peace, as he awaits the anticipated destruction of Nineveh.

The bush, however, has a much more important role to play than simply improving Jonah's mood. The bush is to teach Jonah something about the ways of God and the transitory nature of life. For this bush springs up in a day and it dies the next. In the time that it exists, it serves Jonah well, but such pleasures never last. They are a comfort while present, but not to be trusted to remain. As Ecclesiastes reminds us, we should enjoy such earthly pleasures while they last, for like the wind they pass away.[24]

So the next morning, with the help of a worm, God continues teaching Jonah a lesson. Like the bush, the worm is appointed to serve a particular task. Like the bush, it is only doing what it is designed to do, but it is doing it at God's behest. Chewing the plant causes it to wither, and with the withering, Jonah's shade disappears. "Here today, gone tomorrow," we could say of the bush.

But the story does not end here. There is to be another player in this drama: God sends a sultry east wind. Not being alive in the same way as the worm and the plant, it isn't appointed, but being a creature of God, it does as God commands: it blows mightily, increasing Jonah's discomfort. The sun, also a player in this drama, beats down fiercely on Jonah's head.

Overcome by the heat, the sun, and the sultry wind, Jonah grows faint. Miserable, he recalls his earlier wish to die. Not only is he a laughingstock for claiming that Nineveh will end, but now he is also in great physical discomfort as well. It's obvious that God is playing with him again, just as God had manipulated him in the first place. The whole sorry story is just too much to bear, and he, from the depths of his despair, wishes to die.

Sometimes, even when we think that we are following God's will, all that we have planned seems to fall to pieces. It isn't hard to blame God for the situations in which we find ourselves. In return for our efforts, surely God should treat us better.

After I had finally accepted my call to ordained ministry, I found that I would need to move. Having been in college continuously, first as an undergraduate and then as a graduate student, I was told that I needed to get a job and "experience real life" first. I did find a job, but it was in Lexington, Kentucky. At that point, women could not be ordained priests in that diocese. In order to get a job (which was the next step in the ordination process), I would have to move to a place where it would be impossible for me to continue in the process at all. I felt very much like Jonah as he sat on the hill above Nineveh, in the sweltering heat, and watched all of what he had worked so hard to accomplish crumble in the dust. Why, God, why? Why is all of this necessary?

Yet, of all the characters in these few verses, it's only Jonah who lapses into despair. The rest—plant and worm, wind and sun—all accept God's call unquestioningly. The plant does not protest when it lives for only one day. The worm placidly eats the plant that it is given without questioning if that is really the right thing to do. The wind blows and the sun beats down, fully expressing both their own nature and God's will for them.

It is only we human beings who resist God's will for us so firmly. It is only humans who think that they should be able to direct the way God arranges the world. It is only humans who think that life is not worth living if we are not in charge. It is only we who need to be convinced that we are creatures just like the plant and the worm. It is we who have to learn the hard lessons about trusting that God really knows what is best.

It is not a lesson that we learn easily. It is one that needs to be reinforced in us over and over again. God uses all kinds of things to remind us of this truth that we would just as soon not acknowledge. I suspect that each of us, at some point in our lives, has encountered the plant, the worm, the sun, and the sultry east wind.

Chapter 19

Angry Enough to Die

Jonah 4:9

JONAH did not plant the bush. He did not water the bush. He did not even prune it. The bush is grace. It is a gift, pure and simple, but instead of accepting it as a gift, he sees it as his right. It becomes for him a sign of his privileged position. Sitting high on the hill outside of Nineveh, waiting for the next act of the divine drama, he is given tickets to the box seats, not the bleachers. With the bush shading him, he can wait and watch in comfort.

But the bush is not something that he has earned. It isn't his right to have it to offer him shade. It is a gift given for a time, and as suddenly and abruptly as it appeared, it wilts.

Jonah's reaction to its demise seems all out of proportion to what happens. Why should the loss of shade make him wish to die? Certainly he is hot and miserable, but dying seems an extreme response to a temporary condition. Eventually the sun will sink below the horizon. The evening breezes will begin to blow, and the air will cool. Jonah may be miserable, but it is a problem that will last only a few hours. Death is permanent.

Jonah's response indicates that he feels that he is losing something more important than the shade of the bush. He is losing that which had marked him as special, separate. He is losing that which confirmed, at least in his own mind, the rightness of his actions and beliefs. In the withering of that one bush, Jonah's whole sense of the world and his place in it come crashing down yet again.

How little it takes sometimes to demolish our sense of our own worth. We place our trust in such shaky supports. In the words of Isaiah, we rely on broken reeds.[25] Sometimes, as in the case of Jonah, it is a bush that provides shade from the heat of the day. Unsure of our place and our worth, we grasp for the trappings that confirm, at least in our own minds, that we have value. Possessions, high salaries, special parking places, and the applause of crowds—all of these outward signs become vitally important, so important that the loss of a job, or a perk, or an opportunity, can feel like death.

Such was the loss that I felt when I came close to flunking out of graduate school. For most of my life, my identity and my worth had rested upon my ability to excel academically. It was an area in which I had never failed. In fact, I had never even had to worry about failing. I studied and I worked hard, but I knew that as long as I did, I would always excel. When I finally found a subject in which despite all my hard work I could not do this, it felt like a death.

It was a death. It was the death of my being able to claim value based on academic excellence. It was the death of my self-identity, and in that death I felt lost, cut off from all that had given my life meaning and worth.

Such times in our lives are times of disillusionment. We live with many illusions. We find our worth and meaning in things that can never really guarantee worth and meaning. We especially cling to things that provide no real security, and as long as our illusions remain undisturbed, we may feel a measure of peace and serenity.

The problem with illusions, however, is that they are as fragile as the soap bubbles that children blow. As beautiful as they are, they last only the shortest of moments. As soon as they touch the hard surface of real life, they burst, leaving only a memory. We become disillusioned, and that disillusionment is a form of death.

In the midst of Jonah's disillusionment, his grief, and his calls for death, God is offering another possibility. Instead of the soap bubbles that Jonah has been relying upon, God is offering real worth and real security. Jonah cannot yet see past his anger, to the new life that God is offering him. He cannot see that the loss of the bush does not decrease his value.

As stubborn, as cantankerous, as disobedient, as pigheaded as he is, Jonah is still loved by God. We might have trouble seeing why God bothers with Jonah. At times, we wonder how God can love those whom we have trouble loving. In times of great distress, we may even wonder how God could possibly love us. But God does. We are of inestimable value, for we are God's beloved children. Whatever may happen to us, we are securely held in God's arms. That is a worth and a security that no amount of money, no amount of status, no earthly power can ever match. For money, possessions, and power, can all be stripped from us by others, but God's love and security can never be taken away.

It is tough, leaving our illusions behind, and moving into that place where we live in the light of what is real and true. It can be scary, for it feels like death, but as God has shown us through the cross and Resurrection, that which seems like death can indeed be the way to new life.

Jonah is being offered new life. We do not know whether he will take that gift or whether he will try to replace his shattered illusions with new ones. Like Jonah, the choice is always before us. Where shall we look for our worth and our security, in bushes or in the one who caused the bush to grow and to die?

Chapter 20

What about Nineveh?

Jonah 4:10–11

WHILE Jonah was angry about a plant, the life of Nineveh still hung in the balance. While Jonah was concerned with one life—the life of a plant that lived but one day—God was concerned with the lives of a whole city full of people. While Jonah grieved the death of the plant, God was working to save the lives of more than 120,000 people.

We focus easily on those things that affect our personal lives. The plant affects Jonah directly and personally. It serves Jonah, and Jonah cares about it. The people of Nineveh, however, are beyond Jonah's day-to-day life. Once Jonah leaves Nineveh, he has no more concern for its people. He had never wanted any contact with them, and as far as he is concerned, he is done with them.

God's care and concern, however, extend beyond our limited sight. Where we are blinded by the objects and persons in the foreground of our lives, God sees the long view. In that view, it isn't just Jonah and the plant that he cherishes that matter, but the whole of creation. What Jonah cannot understand is that God loves him, the plant, *and* the people of Nineveh.

How hard it is for us to see that others are also loved by God. It is hard to believe that we are God's cherished children and still believe that God also cares for those for whom we have no care. It is difficult to believe that God loves our enemies as well as us. It is hard to believe that God cares little for the lines that we have drawn. It is hard to believe that God doesn't love us exclusively.

"Does it make sense for you to be worried about a plant?" God asks Jonah. "Yes, it does," Jonah shoots back. "Then why doesn't it make sense to you that I would be concerned about Nineveh? After all, there are more than 120,000 people, those unable to tell their right hand from their left. How can I not reach out to them as well?"

We don't know how Jonah responds to that piece of God's reasoning, for we are at the end of the story. Actually, though, God throws in one final line. When reason cannot reach us, sometimes humor can. Here we see God having the last word with his reluctant prophet. "Well, if you don't care about all those people, what about the cattle?"

Perhaps Jonah was finally able to see the humor. At least I hope so. The ability to appreciate the ridiculous in our lives and in ourselves is one of God's greatest gifts. Did Jonah finally laugh at himself? I hope he found that blessing.

The next time that you find yourself feeling self-righteous and condemning others, remember the absurdity of life, and ask yourself God's question to Jonah. "What about the cattle?"

Chapter 21

What Next?

THE story ends with a question. What about all the cattle, not to mention the more than 120,000 people in the city of Nineveh? If Jonah has an answer to that question it is not recorded.

We can, of course, speculate what Jonah's answer might have been. Based on his earlier responses, we might expect Jonah to be unmoved by the thought. The man who sat on the hillside outside of the city waiting and hoping for its destruction would hardly be expected to care about even the cattle that might be destroyed.

We might hope that all that Jonah has experienced has transformed him into a compassionate, loving human being. Surely with God all things are possible, even the transformation of as difficult a person as Jonah. If that is the case, however, it is left for another story.

Jonah is changed by his call. He changes quite dramatically, in fact. He learns a thing or two about God and about himself. He learns that he isn't quick enough to outrun God. He learns that if God wants him to go someplace, it is probably better to concede defeat and go. He learns that as much as he wants to be in complete control of his life that is impossible.

In fulfilling his calling, however reluctantly, Jonah is changed and transformed. He can never return to his previous life. Too many assumptions about the way that life works have been challenged. Too many illusions have been shattered. Too much has happened to the man from Gath-hepher. He has traveled too far and seen too much.

Our call does not leave us unchanged. Whether we accept it or reject it, we are marked forever. Like the risen Jesus, marked with the signs of the crucifixion, we are also marked.[26] Like Jacob after his struggle with the man in the night, we may forever limp.[27]

My call to ordained ministry changed me, as did the many other calls, large and small, that I have experienced throughout my life. I am forever marked by the ways in which God has chosen to call me. There have been times when I wondered just what God was doing in my life. I have had some very difficult times in the places to which I have been called. I have wondered if perhaps there might be other ways of living out my priesthood. I carry with me the scars and the limps of my struggles with God. Although there may be times when I might wish to return to an earlier time of my life, I cannot. Like Jacob who was renamed Israel, that encounter with God changed my identity. Through this journey, reluctant as I was when I began it, I have become a priest. I am no longer the person whom I once was.

Some people are blessed by knowing what they are called to do from any early age. As long as he can remember, my father wanted to be a veterinarian. Although his family encouraged him to become a "real" doctor, he never let that deter him from his call.

For the rest of us, however, discerning our call may not be so simple and straightforward. We may feel pulled this way and that. We may be much more conflicted about our call. And yet, as painful and as difficult as my call to ordained ministry has sometimes been, I cannot imagine doing anything else. At its best, my call touches something deep inside of me and forces me to become more deeply myself.

Although our call changes us, it does not make us perfect. Like Jonah, we are transformed only in part; there is much of us that is still in need of transformation. Even after Jonah preached to Nineveh in response to his call, he was not immediately made into a compassionate and loving human being. Even after responding to that call, he remained selfish, self-centered, and unbearably self-righteous. He was not an "ideal" man of God.

God, however, isn't finished with him yet. Even at the end of the story there is another call for him to respond to. God is calling him again, this time to an even greater and more difficult ministry. God is calling him to a life of service to and compassion for others. God is calling him to a deeper transformation.

Likewise, God continues to call us. God's calls to me didn't stop with ordination. Marriage, motherhood, writing: each of these calls has helped to mold and to shape me in new ways. Like Jonah, however, there is much in me that is still in need of transformation. There have been and will continue to be calls, calls to service and calls to grow ever more fully into the person whom God has called me to be. Like Jonah, we may prefer to sit in the shade and watch, but as the people of God, we are called to do and to be so much more.

At the end of the book of Jonah, it is clear that Jonah has some more growing to do, but the story also reminds each of us that we need to continue to grow in the love of God. Such growth in the love of God is the call that encompasses all of our individual calls. If I am really honest with myself and with God, I too am far from the person God calls me to be. God is at work in me, and in all of us, to transform us so that we might show forth God's image and glory. "And all of us, with unveiled faces, seeing the glory of the Lord as though reflected in a mirror, are being transformed into the same image from one degree of glory to another; for this comes from the Lord, the Spirit."[28]

Such stories of transformation may sound unbelievable, as unbelievable as the stories of the big fish that are forever eluding the grasp of fishermen and women. These stories, however, have something in common with the more ordinary fish stories, for they acknowledge that something greater lies just beyond our grasp. They speak of joy and sorrow, frustration and triumph. At their best, both stories of transformation and fish stories draw us ever deeper into the search for the "big fish" that we can never land, only admire and pursue with all of our passion, moving ever closer and catching glimpses of our heart's desire.

Like Jonah, we will never catch that big fish. It will remain just beyond our grasp—or, if we are especially blessed, it will swallow us up instead. In the meantime, God has a lot of fish stories to tell in my life and in yours.

Questions for Discussion

Chapter 1

1. Our previous experiences of biblical stories influence how we understand them. Jonah is well known to many people because of its popularity in children's Bibles and storybooks. What did you learn about the book of Jonah as a child? How might that influence the way you understand that big fish story now?

2. Each of us, by virtue of our baptism, is called to follow Christ and to do God's work in the world. Although we share that general call with all Christians, we are each called, individually, to live it out in different ways. What are some of the calls that you have heard in your lifetime? Has God ever called you using someone else's voice?

3. Thinking back over the calls that you identified in question two, how have these calls come out of your passion? How have they responded to the needs of the world?

Chapter 2

1. How do you understand the difference between fact and truth? Can you illustrate the difference with examples?

2. Which is most important to you, to be able to affirm that
    the Bible is factual or that it is true? Why is that important?
3. Share a story that has been important in your life (either
    a piece of fiction or one that contains legendary elements).
    What truth(s) does it convey to you?

Chapter 3

1. Review the list of calls that you generated in discussing
    chapter one. For which of these calls did your skills and
    experience uniquely qualify you?
2. Jonah's call to Nineveh was unwelcome and so distasteful
    to him that he fled, rather than accept it. Recollect a call
    that was scary or even repugnant to you.
3. At times, we each avoid things that we feel that we
    "ought" to be doing. Some of these urges are calls and
    some may be misplaced senses of duty. What ways have
    you used to avoid those things that you did not want to
    do? When did you use the excuse of busyness to avoid
    responding to a deeper call?
4. Calls rarely go away if we ignore them. Instead, they may
    become louder and more persistent. Which calls have you
    been unable to ignore?

Chapter 4

1. When have you tried to limit God's control over you, per-
    haps by keeping parts of your life separate from your faith?
    Why was it important to keep God out?
2. Often our prayers contain those issues that we want God's
    help to solve. Other issues may be completely missing
    from our life of prayer. What issues or parts of your life
    have you been reluctant to bring to God in prayer?

3. When Jonah refused to follow God's call, others suffered. When has your refusal to listen to God caused a storm around you that affected other people?

Chapter 5

1. It can be very difficult to admit our guilt, especially when things go badly. Often we are tempted to remain silent. Have there been times when you should have spoken out and accepted responsibility, but instead remained silent? Was your part ever discovered? If so, how was it uncovered?

2. In times of great distress, we often cry out, "Why?" When have there been times in your life that you have needed to demand why from God? How have you been answered?

3. The word *worship* comes from the Old English word meaning to "assign worth." We worship that which we most highly value. Think of a time in your life when something or someone has been more important to you than God. What did you worship?

Chapter 6

1. We can be caught in the storms caused by someone else's actions, much as the crew was caught in the storm caused by Jonah's disobedience. When have you felt that you have been caught up in someone else's storm? How did you respond?

2. Remember a time when you continued in some action, knowing it was fruitless, simply because the alternatives seemed unthinkable. What changed your mind in the end?

3 In spite of the fact that Jonah was the cause of their distress, the crew tried everything in its power to save him. How have other people risked themselves to save you from the consequences of your own actions?

Chapter 7

1. Have you ever been in a situation when all the possibilities seemed evil? What did you do to try to make it come out all right?
2. When finally forced to make a decision, how did you decide which alternative to choose?
3. In such situations, where do you find God?

Chapter 8

1. When have you faced death? What did you think about in those moments? How did the experience affect your views about your life?
2. Each of us encounters moments in our lives that profoundly change us and make it impossible to return to life the way we previously knew it. What have been some of those occasions in your life?
3. Remember a time when you were caught in a ridiculous situation that was not of you own making. How easy was it to laugh at yourself and the circumstances?

Chapter 9

1. Recollect a time when you felt trapped in a situation where there was no hope of rescue. How did you react?
2. Jonah waited in silence for three days in the belly of the whale. When have you been forced to wait in silence for whatever was to come next?
3. Times of darkness often precede major points of transition in our lives. When have you encountered times of darkness in your own life? How have your times of darkness prepared you for something new?

Chapter 10

1. God does not always answer our prayers in the way that we would hope or expect. What are some of the surprising answers that you have received in response to prayer?
2. In which of those times have you (in retrospect) been glad that God did not answer them as you had requested?
3. How comfortable are you with giving up control of your life to God, especially when your life is not going as you hope or expect?

Chapter 11

1. In the belly of the big fish, Jonah was completely alone. When was a time when you felt cut off from everyone else, even God?
2. In the midst of such times, prayer can be difficult. Have there been times when you could not pray at all? What did you do?
3. Sometimes, we need some time in quiet to be able to identify our deepest desires. It took Jonah three days in the belly of the fish to be able to express his desires. What longings or desires are you aware of at this time in your life?

Chapter 12

1. Sometimes God's call to a specific ministry is clear and we have little choice but to obey. After being spit up on land, Jonah once again heard the call to go to Nineveh. How would you feel under such circumstances? Relieved? Angry? Happy? Resentful?
2. During difficult times, we sometimes long to turn back. What has kept you moving forward in the direction that God was calling you through times of trial?

3. A call can require great sacrifice on our part. Jonah had to give up his desire to direct the course of his life. What have you had to sacrifice in order to follow a call?

Chapter 13

1. When Jonah arrived at Nineveh, the task before him must have seemed overwhelming. How was he to preach to such a large city? When have you been called to an enormous task like Jonah?

2. There are times when, like Jonah, we hope to be overlooked. Perhaps we are embarrassed by the task to which we have been called. Maybe we are even frightened by the possible outcomes. As you have tried to follow God's call, think of some times when you hoped, deep down, that no one would notice what you were doing. Were you able to avoid notice? What happened when you were noticed?

3. Think about the potential problems that you identified as you began to envision living out a call. Which things that you imagined (if any) actually happened? How did your vision of your call match the reality?

Chapter 14

1. The people of Nineveh responded in a way that Jonah could not imagine. They took seriously God's call to repentance. What surprising results have you experienced as you have lived out a call?

2. Jonah was not particularly happy about the response of the Ninevites. Have you ever been unhappy with the response of others to your ministry? What happened and what would you have liked to happen?

3. Have you ever felt the need to beg God's forgiveness in your life the way that the Ninevites did? How do you understand God's judgment and God's forgiveness?

Chapter 15

1. The people of Nineveh were able, through Jonah's preaching, to realize that a change of heart was desperately needed. Their response was wholehearted. What have you heard or who have you encountered that caused you to reevaluate your life in such a dramatic way? How did you respond?
2. The Ninevites were surprised by God's forgiveness. When have you experienced such forgiveness in your own life?
3. At times, God's ways can seem strange and even shocking. Like Jonah, we may not always approve of the way God arranges things. When have you been less than pleased with God's response? Did that response make more sense later on?

Chapter 16

1. Jonah became very angry with God, when God did not follow through with God's threats. Jonah even yelled at God. What typically causes you to become angry with God? How do you handle your anger with God?
2. "God delights in turning upside down all our thoughts that we might have about our call." Have you ever experienced such upheaval in your sense of call? What was the result of having your life turned upside down?
3. When we are angry or upset with God, we often feel cut off from God. Prayer can be difficult. When have you found it difficult to pray to God?

Chapter 17

1. At times, our anger seems justified. Jonah felt that he had the right to be angry when God did not destroy Nineveh as promised. When have you felt justified in your anger at God?
2. Name some times when God did not answer your prayers in the way that you would have wished. How did those times affect your relationship with God?
3. Our anger can cause us to be blind to the workings of God around us. Think back on times when you may have been angry with God. Were there things that you did not notice in your anger?

Chapter 18

1. God can work through anything, including a bush, a worm, and a sultry east wind. Have there been times when you have seen God at work in things in the world around you?
2. Jonah seemed to take the plant for granted, as something due him for his service to God. How do you view what you have been given? Do you deserve what you have or is it a gift?
3. When his world crumbled around him, Jonah wished that he could die. When have you wished that you could die?

Chapter 19

1. The bush that shaded Jonah was pure gift. He had not planted the seed. He did not water the seedling. He was not in any way responsible for its growth. It simply appeared. Think back over your own life. What things come to mind that you received that were pure gift?

2. In a short time, Jonah's bush had become very important to him. In fact, the loss of that bush sent him into
   despair. What have you lost that drove you to despair like
   Jonah?
3. We have many illusions. We have illusions about ourselves
   and our abilities. We have illusions about other people. Perhaps one of our biggest illusions is that we are in control of
   our own lives. We tend to hold tightly onto our illusions
   until something smashes them. When have you become
   disillusioned, and what caused that disillusionment?

Chapter 20

1. Often our own concerns and worries block us from being
   aware of the greater problems in the world around us.
   What concerns or worries do you have that tend to make
   you blind to those around you who may be suffering?
2. If we are honest with ourselves, most of us cannot really
   believe that certain people are loved by God. Perhaps we
   include in that list historical characters of great cruelty.
   Maybe there are people we know who are so unpleasant
   that we cannot really imagine how God could possibly
   love them. Who do you find it difficult to believe that
   God really loves?
3. At the end of the book of Jonah, God uses humor to reach
   out to Jonah. When have you encountered God's sense of
   humor?

Chapter 21

1. Jonah's call changed Jonah quite dramatically. He had to
   learn many lessons, chief among them was that God is
   really in control of his life. What lessons have you learned

as you have listened for and tried to respond to (or avoid) God's call in your life?

2. Although our previous call may give us some hint of the direction in which God is calling us now, God can indeed be surprising. As Jonah found out, God can call us to places that we never intended to go. Where do you hear God's call at this point in your life? How will you respond to that call?

3. Our ultimate call is to draw ever closer to that big fish that always eludes our grasp. What helps you to catch glimpses of it in the shadows?

☀ Endnotes ☀

1. *The Book of Common Prayer* (New York: Church Hymnal Corporation, 1979), p. 305.

2. Frederick Buechner, *Wishful Thinking: A Theological ABC* (New York: Harper & Row Publishers, 1973), p. 95.

3. Genesis 32:22–32.

4. Exodus 4:10–17.

5. Matthew 13:34.

6. 2 Kings 14:25.

7. 1 Samuel 3:1–18; Isaiah 6:1–8; Luke 1:26–38.

8. Genesis 15; Judges 6:36–40.

9. Isaiah 7:10–14.

10. Exodus 4:10–12.

11. Jeremiah 1:4–8.

12. Hebrews 10:31.

13. 1 Samuel 14:36–46.

14. Genesis 3:8–10.

15. Annie Dillard, *Teaching a Stone to Talk* (New York: Harper & Row Publishers, 1982), pp. 40–41.

16. Jonah 1:9b.

17. John 8:32.

18. John 5:2–9.

19. Exodus 14.

20. Genesis 6:5–8.

21. Exodus 32:7–10.

22. Genesis 9:1–7.

23. Genesis 3.

24. Ecclesiastes 2:24–26.

25. Isaiah 36:6.

26. John 20:24–27.

27. Genesis 32:22–32.

28. 2 Corinthians 3:18.

About the Author

TARA SOUGHERS is the author of *Falling in Love with God: Passion, Prayer, and the Songs of Songs*, and she is currently completing a book about finding God in times of darkness. All of her works explore the many ways in which we encounter God in our daily lives (whether we want to or not), and the ways in which we are transformed by those encounters. Biblical narratives and personal stories are used to illuminate a variety of paths to God, and readers are invited to consider their own stories of transformation.

Soughers is a spiritual director and parish priest. She has served parishes in Utah, New York, Connecticut, and Massachusetts. She lives in Wrentham, Massachusetts, with her husband, Mike, and her children, Arielle and Gregory, where she tries to listen for God in the midst of the busyness of everyday life.